SQL

SELF-TEACHING GUIDE

Wiley SELF-TEACHING GUIDES (STG's) are designed for first time users of computer applications and programming languages. They feature concept-reinforcing drills, exercises, and illustrations that enable you to measure your progress, and learn at your own pace. Other Wiley Self-Teaching Guides:

DOS 5 STG, Ruth Ashley and Judi N. Fernandez
INTRODICTION TO PERSONAL COMPUTERS STG, Peter Stephenson
OBJECTIVISION STG, Arnold and Edith Shulman
QUATTRO PRO 3 STG, Jennifer Meyer
LOTUS 1-2-3 FOR WINDOWS STG, Douglas J. Wolf
PARADOX 3.5 STG, Gloria Wheeler
Q&A 4 STG, Corey Sandler and Tom Badgett
FOXPRO 2 STG, Ellen Sander
ALDUS PERSUASION FOR IBM PC'S AND COMPATIBLES STG, Karen Brown and Diane Stielstra
PERFORM STG, Peter Stephenson
NOVELL NETWARE 2.2 STG, Peter Stephenson and Glenn Hartwig
MICROSOFT WORD 5.5 FOR THE PC STG, Ruth Ashley and Judi Fernandez
MICROSOFT WORD FOR WINDOWS 2 STG, Pamela S. Beason and Stephen Guild
WORDPERFECT 5.0/5.1 STG, Neil Salking
SIGNATURE STG, Christine Rivera
MICROSOFT WINDOWS 3.0 STG, Keith Weiskamp and Saul Aguiar
PC DOS 4 STG, Ruth Ashley and Judi Fernandez
PC DOS 3.3 STG, Ruth Ashley and Judi Fernandez
MASTERING MICROSOFT WORKS STG, David Sachs, Babette Kronstadt, Judith Van Wormer, and Barbara Farrell
QUICKPASCAL STG, Keith Weiskamp and Saul Aguiar
GW BASIC STG, Ruth Ashley and Judi Fernandez
TURBO C++ STG, Bryan Flamig
QUICKEN STG, Peter Aitken
COREL DRAW 2 STG, Robert Bixby
HARVARD GRAPHICS 3 STG, David Harrison and John W. Yu
HARVARD GRAPHICS FOR WINDOWS STG, David Harrison and John W. Yu
AMI PRO 2 FOR WINDOWS STG, Pamela S. Beason and Stephen Guild

To order our STG's, you can call Wiley directly at (201) 469-4400, or check your local bookstores.

"Mastering computers was never this easy, rewarding, and fun!"

SQL

SELF-TEACHING GUIDE

Peter Stephenson
Glenn Hartwig

John Wiley & Sons

New York ▲ Chichester ▲ Brisbane ▲ Toronto ▲ Singapore

Copyright © 1992 by Peter Stephenson and Glenn Hartwig

Library of Congress Cataloging-in-Publication Data
Stephenson, Peter, 1944-
    SQL: self-teaching guide/Peter Stephenson, Glenn Hartwig
      p. cm.
    Includes index.
    ISBN 0-471-54544-9
    1. SQL (Computer program language) I. Hartwig, Glenn II. Title
    QA76.73.S67S74 1992
    005.13'3—dc20   92-7098

Printed in the United States of America

10 9 8 7 6 5 4 3

Contents Overview

Contents

Introduction

Welcome to the world of SQL. SQL (or, Structured Query Language) originated on large platforms—mainframes and minicomputers—and has only recently begun to be popular on PCs. There are several books available that discuss SQL from the perspective of large scale implementations on particular platforms. SQL does, however, have a common core that, generally, is available in all implementations. This core provides the foundation for database creation and use on all platforms for which SQL products are available.

In this book we will not tackle the extensions of SQL. Instead, we will concentrate on the basics that are common to virtually all SQL implementations. The idea is that, once you master this book, you'll be able to use just about any SQL system and, for the effort of learning its differences, master it as well. For our model, we have chosen SQLBase from Gupta Technologies, Inc., in Menlo Park, California. SQLBase uses the command set implemented by IBM's DB2 and Oracle as well as many additional commands unique to the Gupta product. We are concerned, however, only with the ANSI (American National Standards Institute) standard SQL portion of the program. Code examples are used by permission of the copyright owner, Gupta Technologies, Inc.

How to Use This Self-Teaching Guide

Each chapter includes sections that cover specific topics and features. In addition, the following tools have been provided to make the most of your learning time:

Check Yourself sections include a short, hands-on practice exercise that can be performed on your own computer. Each chapter includes several of these sections, which will help you to learn by performing specific tasks. These ensure that you understand one topic before moving on to the next, and allow you to learn at your own pace.

Practice What You've Learned sections are found at the end of each chapter. They provide another way to check your knowledge, and cover the key topics presented in the chapter. These longer exercises include instructions for you to follow, and responses from the program that detail what you should be seeing on the screen as you perform each step.

Tip sections appear throughout the book, helping to draw your attention to special features and shortcuts. They also offer suggestions for using the features you have learned about. Incorporating these tips into your normal routine enables you to work at the most productive level, and shortens the time needed to perform tasks.

Quick Summaries fall at the end of each chapter, and review any shortcut keys, tasks, and procedures covered in the chapter.

Conventions

ALL CAPS   All caps indicate text you must type on your keyboard. You can type it in uppercase, lowercase, or a mixture of both.

[Square brackets]   Information in square brackets is variable. You will enter information such as table names based on your own names for those tables.

Key + key   Two or more key names connected by a plus sign (+) indicates that you should press those keys simultaneously.

Trademarks

SQLBase, SQLWindows, and SQLTalk are trademarks of Gupta Technologies, Inc.

IBM, IBM PC, IBM Extended Edition 1.2 Database Manager, SQL/DS, and DB2 trademarks of International Business Machines Corporation.

UNIX is a registered trademark of AT&T.

Microsoft, Microsoft SQL Server, MS-DOS, OS/2, and Windows 3.0 are registered trademarks of Microsoft Corporation.

VAX is a registered trademark of Digital Equipment Corporation.

Oracle, SQLPLUS, SQLNET, and Oracle Server are registered trademarks of Oracle Corp.

Paradox and Paradox SQL Link are registered trademarks of Borland International, Inc.

dBASE is a registered trademark and dBASE III and dBASE IV are trademarks of Ashton-Tate Corp.

The Relational
Database

SQL, the structured query language, is based upon a special kind of database called a relational database. Many database management programs in today's PC world claim to be relational, but, actually, are not. In order for a database management program to truly use SQL, it must follow the relational model very closely. In this chapter you will learn about relational databases and how relationality affects SQL. This chapter covers:

▲ **The relational model**

▲ **The importance of relationality**

▲ **Concurrency control and data integrity**

▲ **How to determine if a database is relational**

What Is the Relational Model?

SQL is based upon the relational model of data. As we pointed out in the introduction to this chapter, many databases call themselves relational. Actually, very few are. In fact, there are those purists who insist that there are no truly relational database management systems (DBMSs). We won't argue that point here, but we will give you some insight as to why these DBMS mavens make the statement.

In the first place, successful use of SQL depends upon the relationality of the database. Some years ago E. F. Codd, then an employee of IBM, presented a schema for the relational database. Codd is considered to be the "father" of the relational database. There were, in his defining statement, some 12 rules for relationality. In addition, he included a 13th rule he called the zero rule because he felt that it preceded all of the others. However, for practical purposes, these 13 rules are overkill.

C. J. Date, an associate of Codd during the relational databases definitive years, subsequently simplified the definition of the relational model considerably. In his view, there was a subset of Codd's rules that was sufficient to define the requirements of a relational database. The remaining rules, he believed, were merely "nice to have." For our purposes, since there is considerable sophisticated mathematics associated with Codd's 12 rules, we'll stick with the Date approach.

Before we get too deeply into our discussion of relationality, we need to change your vocabulary a bit. Many of the terms you are used to in normal PC database parlance are not really appropriate

▼ *Table 1.1. Some Relational Database Terms*

Formal Relational Term	Informal	Nonrelational
Relation	Table	Database
Tuple	Row	Record
Attribute	Column	Field

to relational-speak. Table 1.1 shows you the formal terminology, the informal terminology (which we'll use in this book), and the approximate nonrelational equivalents for three terms.

Relational database management systems also have databases; however, they are made up of tables. The tables are roughly equivalent to nonrelational databases. Generally, a relational database consists of several tables of data that can be connected to form additional, virtual tables. We'll discuss that process and what it means in Chapter 3. Now on to some of the important rules. We could, presumably, consider the definition of a relational database to proceed from these rules.

First, and most important, a relational database must be perceived as a collection of tables of data and nothing but tables of data. That means that "cells" in the tables can't be formulas or pointers to other tables. We refer to a database system with this architecture (i.e., consisting of tables and nothing but tables) as being tabular. The links between tables must be created by virtue of common data, not by virtue of intertable links. An outgrowth of this rule is that data stored in the table is atomic in nature. That means that the data in a cell (the intersection of a row and a column) is the smallest unit in the table. There cannot be two pieces of data in a cell. Also, again growing out of this rule, each table has a primary key.

A key is a column in a table from which you can order the rest of the values in the table. The primary key is valid if at any given time no row of any column other than the column you select for the key has the same value as the same row in the column you select for the primary key. When you order the rows based upon the primary key you are said to be indexing the table, or creating an index. You cannot have a null value (an empty cell) as a primary key.

There is another type of key called a foreign key. The foreign key is a key in another table that matches the primary key in the base table. (The base table is the one that contains real data—there are also virtual or result tables that are created when you combine more than one base table. We'll discuss result tables in more detail when we discuss the use of multiple SQL tables.) In order for a foreign key to be valid for a particular base table, every one of its values must exactly match a value of the primary key in the base table. That status is called referential integrity and is another property of relational databases. We'll learn more about referential integrity and keys later in this chapter in the subsection on data integrity.

Finally, in order to be minimally relational, a database management system must support the relational algebra for the basic query operations SELECT, PROJECT, and JOIN without requiring any predefinition of physical access paths. That means that the system cannot require the user to create formulas or commands to produce the results of the SELECT, PROJECT, or JOIN operations. They must be supported directly by the system itself. It is not necessary to have these functions as specific commands, as long as their functionality is correctly supported.

Relational algebra is a special branch of boolean mathematics that deals with the rules for dealing with relational databases. Its study is certainly beyond our scope here except to point out that, unlike other branches of database theory, relational algebra is concerned with set theory. That means that as we collect, collate, and correlate data in the SQL database, we are actually creating sets of data. The process for creating these data sets is well defined using the rules of relational algebra.

As we continue our discussions and become familiar with the selection of data from tables, you will notice that we are, in fact, selecting sets of data in conformance with the queries we create. The queries define the requirements that a piece of data in a table must meet in order to be included in the data set. The underlying code supporting the commands in our query was created to support the boolean mathematics of relational algebra. Any command whose underlying code does not support that algebra cannot assure that you are accurately choosing data. In a true SQL database system supporting true relational databases, the commands are always derived from relational algebra.

TIP

If a database management system does not support relational algebra, it is not relational. Thus, it cannot use real SQL commands even if its commands look like SQL.

CHECK YOURSELF

1. What familiar nonrelational terms are the same as table, row, and column?

2. Name the two most important requirements for a database to be relational.

3. What is a key?

ANSWERS

1. A relational table is similar to a nonrelational database, a row is similar to a record, and a column is similar to a field.

2. The data must be viewed as tabular and only tabular, and the database must support the relational algebra for the operations SELECT, PROJECT, and JOIN.

3. A key is a unique column value by which you can order the rows of a table.

Why Is Relationality Important?

Relational database management systems use set theory to define their relationships. As we progress, you will see that not all systems allow complete adherence to the relational model. Interestingly, some popular PC databases are almost relational, or, as C. J. Date calls them, "relational-like." In order to completely support SQL, a system must be at least minimally relational. Otherwise, its use in a distributed system will be difficult, if not impossible.

Some of those PC databases—the relational-like ones—are, actually, pretty close to being relational. In fact some, like dBASE IV SQL, have been enhanced to meet the requirements of a relational database very closely. dBASE IV SQL is, for all practical purposes, a relational system. dBASE has always had a tabular data structure. dBASE IV, however, added several capabilities in its SQL mode that support much of the relational algebra and coincide with some of the early SQL structures such as IBM's DB2 and SQL/DS. Thus, queries formulated in dBASE IV SQL are similar to those found in other legitimate SQL systems.

Even though dBASE IV SQL is a legitimate SQL implementation, it is not necessarily capable of communicating with other SQL systems. SQL syntax (the way you write the language) is not the only aspect to the use of SQL in a distributed environment. In order to query other databases residing on different types of systems, you must also adhere to that system's other parameters. Those parameters include data format and operating system environment. Thus we can't necessarily expect that one SQL system can access data from another.

However, if we stick to the relational model and the core syntax of standard SQL, we'll have no trouble learning different SQL database management systems. In this book we'll use SQLBase as our example. Because it is not only a standard implementation of SQL, but also capable (unlike dBASE IV and other SQL-like programs) of connecting to certain other SQL systems, you'll find that our examples will work on just about any other SQL program you might be using. You'll be able to practice with the language elements and exercises you'll find in this book. If you are using another SQL database, you'll be surprised at how little difference you find between our examples and the actual syntax of your database management system. Feel free to experiment with the exercises in this book on your system. You'll find that, more often than not, they yield the same results on your PC as they do in the pages of this book.

Data Integrity

We gave an example of referential integrity earlier. At that time we mentioned how referential integrity requires that any column in a base table (the table whose data you are referencing elsewhere) that is referenced in another table must exist in the base table and must contain at least every value referenced. To put it in a little different light, here's another way to view it. If you are going to use several tables of data in a database, and you want to form connections between them, you must insure that all of the columns you use in your connections are present in all of the tables involved. Here's an example. Suppose that you want to create a database for an automobile dealership. You would have a table listing the cars you have to sell—in other words, your inventory. You would have a table listing your sales staff. And, finally, you would have a table listing sales made. The tables might have the following structures (the following are the column names for each of the tables):

Why Is Relationality Important?

▼ Table 1.2. Data Structures of Three Sample Tables

The Inventory Table

Make	Model	Color	Cost	Price	IDNum

The Sales Staff Table

Lname	Fname	SSN	Commiss	Emplnum

The Sales Table

CLname	CFname	Saledate	IDNum	Emplnum

Notice that the bulk of the important data in the sales table will come from the other two tables. For example, the IDNum column in the inventory table is the primary key for the same column in the sales table. That makes IDNum in the sales table a foreign key in relation to the inventory table. The same is true for the Emplnum in the sales staff table. It is the primary key for the Emplnum column in the sales table, making sales.Emplnum (a shorthand way of writing the Emplnum column of the sales table) its foreign key.

The customer's last name (CLname) and first name (CFname) as well as the sale date are independent. But the ID number of the car the customer purchased (IDNum) and the employee number of the salesperson who sold the car (Emplnum) came from other tables. In order to have referential integrity, the IDNum and Emplnum columns must exist in the other tables and there must be exactly the same values in those tables that you will reference in the sales table. That is one type of database integrity.

Relative to the sales table, IDNum and Emplnum are considered foreign keys. Within their own tables, they might be the primary keys. In either case, you can create an index based upon the key. In the base tables, it would be quite logical to order the inventory table by the automobile's ID. It would be equally logical to order the sales staff table by employee number. The sales table, however, could logically be ordered by the car sold, the person selling it, or the buyer.

Another type of data integrity is unique to multitable operations. Suppose, in our example above, you are completing your entry in the sales table and it needs to update the salesperson's commission with the sale. The database application would take the price from the inventory table, apply a commission formula to it to calculate the salesperson's commission, and then enter the commission in the sales staff table for the appropriate salesperson. Suppose, for the sake of argument, that in the middle of that action the computer failed and, even though the commission had been calculated, the entry was not made in the sales staff table. This would result in the loss of data integrity. In accounting jargon, the tables would be out of balance with each other.

In an SQL database application there is a solution to this problem. First, the situation we just described is called a transaction and the type of application involved is called a transaction processing application. Each individual transaction consists of a number of steps that the application must perform to complete the transaction. Once the steps have all been completed, the application commits (saves) the transaction. This takes almost no time. Without transaction processing, it could take as long to record and calculate all of the appropriate steps as it does to type the data into the tables. Using transaction processing, the actual database manipulations are done all at once and the amount of time they take depends only upon the speed of the computer and the efficiency of the database system.

While our example is very simple, real database transactions can be highly complex, dealing with many tables across networks. Using the commit, there is minimal chance of a failure interrupting the posting of the transaction. Even so, the application checks to see that the transaction is truly complete before moving on to the next. If it finds that, for whatever reason, the transaction was not completed, the SQL application performs a rollback. A rollback returns all of the tables involved in the transaction to their states just prior to the transaction. Thus, the application maintains data integrity.

TIP

Data integrity is extremely important in relational databases (or any databases, for that matter). However, the mechanisms for maintaining data integrity within a relational database are, perhaps, the most reliable of any of the many types of databases.

While commit and rollback are not considered SQL commands, they are usually part of any expanded SQL syntax. More about that will be discussed a bit later in Chapter 2.

Concurrency Control

Concurrency control is a predominant feature of multiuser SQL systems. Concurrency control refers to the ability of the system to insure that changes made by one user are accessible to all users. Here is the traditional concurrency control problem. Assume that two users, A and B, are logged in to a multiuser SQL system. They are both browsing the same row in the same table. User A, unbeknownst to user B, updates the row. User B, subsequently, decides to update the same row. The row has been changed twice and neither user is aware of the other user's change.

The solution is to notify the second user that a change has been made since he or she logged on to the table. There are a couple of ways to do that. One is to interrupt user B as he or she begins to update. The other is called database refresh. Systems using database refresh periodically scan all of the tables in the database and rewrite any values that have changed and that are currently being browsed. That insures that the user browsing the table will see the most current values.

Another concurrency control problem occurs during batch processes such as indexing. If one user attempts to update or add a row to a table during an indexing procedure, it is possible that he or she will corrupt the index. Thus, the usual solution is to lock any table being indexed against writes during the indexing process. That means that users can browse but not change a table while it is being indexed. Unfortunately, some database systems use what we refer to as brute force locking whenever a user is writing to a database. That means that the entire table is locked, or at least the row in use is locked, for the entire process. The better, and more efficient method is to use transaction processing. Here's an example of what can go wrong when using brute force locking.

User A is working with an SQL database. He or she has a row for browsing and decides to update it. The application locks the row. The phone rings. User A answers. The row is still locked against other users' writes. The conversation takes ten minutes or so and results in a lunch date. User A leaves for lunch. The row is still locked because the user forgot to complete the transaction. It's Friday, so the lunch date lasts for the rest of the day. The row is still locked. Monday, our user is sick and fails to report for work. The row is still locked. Effectively, that part of the table has been out of use for a day and a half.

Had the developer who created the application used transaction processing, the row would never have been locked until the transaction was completed and committed. At that point, the lock would have been under the control of the application and would have lasted but a fraction of a second. If there had been a computer failure during that day and a half, data integrity could have been compromised as well.

CHECK YOURSELF

1. What is referential integrity?

2. What is concurrency control?

3. What is the advantage of transaction processing?

ANSWERS

1. Referential integrity is the concept that any column in a base table that is referenced in another table must exist in the base table and must have available at least every value referenced.

2. Concurrency control is a multiuser concept that dictates that when two or more users are accessing the same row in

a table, changes to that row by one user are reflected to the other users.

3. Transaction processing retains locks on a record for only the briefest time during an update, thus assuring that the row is available as much as possible, and it protects data integrity through the use of commit and rollback.

What Databases Are Relational?

As we said earlier, there are few, if any, completely relational databases. However, in the PC environment, there are a few that come close enough to provide the benefits of a good SQL system. If, however, the basic database structure is not relational in nature, there will be some prices to pay. Chief among these is performance. In addition, data integrity can be suspect.

There have been, in the past, databases that claim relationality by virtue of their supposed ability to use SQL that were, in fact, not relational. One of the major type of pseudorelational databases is the type of system that places an SQL layer over a so-called record manager. Most record managers are, actually, hierarchical database management systems. Hierarchical databases use a system of parent/child relationships. This concept is not relational. Instead it arranges data in a hierarchy where data elements (children) proceed from other elements (parents). The system is not necessarily tabular in nature, nor does it support the relational algebra directly. Thus, in order to use true SQL queries, some translation of the data and its format is necessary to simulate a relational system. This translation violates one of the rules of relationality and results in severely reduced performance.

The idea that an SQL surface can be applied to a nonrelational database structure is not new. In the early days of relational PC databases, many database developers attempted to claim SQL capability simply by using a collection of commands that sounded like SQL. The problem arises when users attempt to perform some of the more complex table joins. A join is a process whereby a result table is created out of the columns of several base tables.

In our earlier example, we created a table (sales) that had elements of a multitable join and its own columns (the first and last names of the buyer). If we had added a third base table, called prospects, for example, which contained all of the potential purchasers and their names, addresses, and phone numbers, we could create the sales table completely from the rows and columns in the other tables. Thus, the sales table would be a result table, also sometimes called a view.

However, this many-to-one relationship is not quite as easy to create in a nonrelational database. Moreover, the results are often suspect. The special nature of the relational database makes the various kinds of joins required by SQL very easy to perform. The alternative is to write special code to bypass the special abilities of the relational database. This code causes serious performance degradation in most cases. However, just because a database is relational doesn't mean that there isn't some code required to make the SQL queries work well. This special code is called an optimizer and the process in which this special code is used is called optimization.

The purpose of optimizing an SQL query is to reduce it from its English language-like syntax to a set of instructions that actually means something to the database. The first step in processing an SQL query is optimization. That doesn't mean, however, that the program translates the query. It simply follows a set of rules for reducing the query language to something useful and then deciding the order in which the database will process the elements of the query. As you will shortly learn, SQL queries are rather complex in their syntax. Building an SQL query is rather like creating a sentence in English. You pile the elements of the sentence upon each other until you have a collection of words and phrases that conveys your meaning.

Good SQL database management programs have three parts. They have the SQL syntax, a set of functions, and a set of procedural commands. If the procedural commands are not present, the database is not programmable. SQL itself is not a programming language. It is, instead, a query language. That means that you can create databases and tables, add, delete, and modify data within them, and request data from them. You must do this by issuing interactive commands called SQL statements. If you want to embed SQL in a program or application, you need some procedural commands to control program flow. SQL statements only control data flow. In the next chapter you'll learn about interactive and embedded SQL.

Currently, there are very few popular SQL database management systems for PCs that can be considered relational. These databases fall into two general categories. The first category, that of distributed database management systems, contains those systems designed from the ground up to be relational SQL systems capable of being used in a multiuser, heterogeneous environment. That's a lot of jargon to swallow, but its meaning is really pretty simple. A heterogeneous database environment is one where the database management system can query, update, add, and delete data from other similar database management systems even if they are different systems. The only requirements are that all of the systems support the relational model, the same subset of the SQL syntax, and are optimized to work with each other.

Some examples of these are Microsoft SQL Server, Gupta Technologies SQLBase, and Oracle Server. These systems can, for the most part, work with each other and the leading mainframe SQL system, IBM's DB2. There are, of course, other, not so well-known products, but these command the largest share of the PC relational database market.

What Databases Are Relational?

What If a Database Is Almost Relational?

There is a second category of SQL systems for PCs. These are, largely, reworked versions of popular single-user products. The first step for most of these systems has been expansion to some form, however crude, of multiuser system. The second step has been the addition of SQL capability. Many of these systems have had to undergo significant translation and optimization to provide even a semblance of real SQL performance. Usually, these systems cannot be used in a heterogeneous environment. When they can, the process is often a bit of a kludge. You'll learn more about that in Chapter 2.

Some of the programs that fit into this category are Ashton-Tate's dBASE IV, Borland's Paradox, and Microrim's R:Base. On all of these the SQL implementation, within the program, is reasonably good. The databases are relational enough so that they work, but without a fair amount of external manipulation, they won't work in a heterogeneous environment.

These almost relational database systems can provide a certain level of benefits under certain circumstances. The main use for these systems is in medium size to small multiuser environments where no connection to a database from another developer ever is anticipated. They provide a level of performance beyond traditional PC database management systems, especially in a networked system. They are, after all, a combination of data handling and program handling. That distinction, by the way, demands a moment of our attention.

Early PC database management systems, such as dBASE III, were very good programming environments from the perspective that they were simple to use and provided a great deal of programmability, especially in the database applications that make up most business requirements. However, for all of their powerful ease of use on the programming side of things (program flow control), they were very weak in their actual handling of data (data flow control). For that reason, when their developers ported them to multiuser systems, which often keep data in several places at the same time, there were severe performance issues to confront.

Most of these confrontations were not particularly elegant or successful. The addition of a closer adherence to real relationality and the use of a real database management language—SQL—added the dimension of data flow control and greatly improved database application performance. However, this came at a cost: the inability to interface directly with other SQL systems from other developers.

However, if you want to obtain better database manipulation and you are operating in a relatively isolated environment, you can certainly take advantage of one of these systems. For example, if you currently are using dBASE III Plus, you can benefit from upgrading to dBASE IV and converting the data-handling portions of your applications to dBASE IV SQL.

Some database management systems are not, however, relational enough to really support SQL in any manner other than the use of the SQL commands.

TIP

Just because a program uses the SQL syntax doesn't mean that it is relational or that the commands are really performing true SQL functions.

"So what?" you ask. "If it walks like a duck and quacks like a duck, take it for a duck." Well, databases aren't ducks and there are a great many that walk and quack like SQL but are not using the techniques that distinguish SQL from other languages. Thus, they don't reap the performance benefits of SQL nor do they have any way of working in even the simplest of heterogeneous environments. If all you need is a simple language, these are not good choices for you. Their simplicity is overshadowed by their lack of relational performance.

QUICK SUMMARY

Here are some of the important points in this chapter. The word or phrase in bold lists a relational database feature. That feature's definition and its benefit to you follows.

Tabular nature All databases must be perceived as tables of data and nothing else. The tabular nature of relational databases enables them to be used in complex SQL queries with full confidence in query results and ease of performing joins.

Atomic nature of data Each data element is a single element and can be identified as such. Prevents ambiguities that can cause errors and improves database performance.

Referential integrity The concept that any column in a base table that is referenced in another table must exist in the base table and must have available at least every value referenced. Allows use of several base tables to produce a result table or view.

Concurrency control A multiuser concept that dictates that, when two or more users are accessing the same row in a table, changes to that row by one user are reflected to the other users. Prevents ambiguities in database tables on a multiuser system.

Transaction processing The ability to condense a transaction into a single action that the application can commit if successful or rollback if unsuccessful. Improves application performance and prevents loss of data integrity.

PRACTICE WHAT YOU'VE LEARNED

Throughout this book you will have chapter end exercises that will help you test your understanding of the material in the chapter. For many of the chapters later in the book, these exercises will consist of formulating a query or two based upon the material covered in the chapter. These chapters (starting with Chapter 4) will cover specific SQL statements for which we will use the syntax in SQLBase. Starting with Chapter 5 you will be able to form the query using SQLBase or your SQL program. If you are using a different SQL implementation, you'll get, perhaps, slightly different results than in this book.

However, for Chapters 1 through 4 we will be discussing concepts. So our exercises will be a little bit different. Generally, we will ask you to discuss some of the concepts we have presented in the chapter. Used with the Check Yourself sections throughout the chapter, these short exercises will help your understanding of SQL.

1. Describe the requirements for a relational database in terms of the relational model.

2. What are some of the benefits to the relational database model?

3. What is data integrity?

4. Describe two typical concurrency control scenarios.

5. Distinguish between relational PC database management systems and "almost relational" or "relational-like" systems.

6. Give some examples of relational databases and almost relational systems.

7. What are the penalties for using a nonrelational system that uses SQL as a query language to give the appearance of ease of use?

ANSWERS

1. A relational database must be perceived as a collection of tables of data and nothing but tables of data. The links between tables must be created by virtue of common data, not by virtue of intertable links. An outgrowth of this rule is that data stored in the table is atomic in nature. That means that the data in a cell (the intersection of a row and a column) is the smallest unit in the table. There cannot be two pieces of data in a cell. Finally, the database must support the relational algebra for the functions SELECT, PROJECT, and JOIN.

2. Relational databases are a requirement for true SQL. Also, the relational model provides excellent controls on data integrity as well as ease of performing multitable queries.

3. Data integrity refers to the consistency of data in tables of a database.

4. One is where two or more users are updating the same row of a table at the same time, unaware of each other. Another is the situation where a user is updating a table at the same time another user is performing an index on it.

5. Relational PC database management systems are usually those that were created as such for use on multiuser heterogeneous databases with SQL as the query language. Relational-like databases are those that have been adapted for use in an SQL environment and have most of, but not all, the characteristics of the relational databases. They cannot easily be used in a heterogeneous database environment.

6. Some relational PC databases are SQLBase, SQL Server, and Oracle Server. Relational-like examples are dBASE IV, Paradox, and R:Base.

7. The primary penalty is performance. There may also be problems with data integrity.

Database Query Techniques

Now that we've learned about the relational model and its importance to an SQL database, it's time to explore the differences between a query language such as SQL and other types of database languages. As we explore different types of database languages, we'll mention, in passing, some of the most widely used database management systems that use those languages. In this chapter you'll learn about:

- ▲ The difference between procedural and nonprocedural languages
- ▲ Query by example (QBE)
- ▲ Interactive SQL
- ▲ Embedded SQL
- ▲ Multiuser issues affecting SQL databases

Procedural and Nonprocedural Languages

Within the realm of database management systems and their individual languages there are two broad categories. These categories, procedural and nonprocedural, define the capabilities, and, thus, the use of the language. All database management systems (DBMS) use one or the other. Some use both.

All languages, regardless of their type or purpose, are made up of common elements. In addition, depending upon the nature of the language, there may be other elements that distinguish it. The common elements, found in all languages, are vocabulary and syntax. Vocabulary, also known as semantics, refers to the commands or statements that make up the language. Syntax refers to the rules for their use.

Procedural languages are those that fit within the boundaries of "traditional" programming languages. They allow you to create a program made up of procedures. In other words, you can store a series of commands into an executable file, or program, that you run to perform some function. Additionally, procedural languages have other features that distinguish them from nonprocedural ones.

Procedural languages are concerned with two types of program management: data flow control and program flow control. The presence of commands or statements in the language's vocabulary that manage program flow control distinguishes the procedural language from the nonprocedural one. Program flow commands are those that control the process of the program. They tell the PC to "do this," "now, do that," "next, if you get this response do this, if not do something else." Simply, they instruct the PC's operating system to execute a series of commands, in a specified order, possibly depending upon the results of some other command or statement.

Data flow commands, on the other hand, are those that are concerned strictly with the addition, deletion, or extraction of data from one or more databases or data tables. They have nothing at all to do with determining the flow of the program. They are only for manipulating data and returning the results of a query. Thus, you can have a language that allows only the manipulation of data.

Such a language would not allow you to create a program that executes a series of commands because it would not have the capability of program flow control. It does not have program flow control commands in its vocabulary. Therefore, such a language would be a nonprocedural language. Query languages are nonprocedural. SQL is a query language and, therefore, is nonprocedural. You cannot write a program in SQL. But, as you will soon see, you can embed SQL in a program written in a procedural language.

Procedural and Nonprocedural Languages

TIP

There are several database languages that combine the characteristics of procedural and nonprocedural languages. These languages, typically considered procedural, attempt to provide the optimum mix of program flow control and data flow control. Unfortunately, most fall short in one or the other.

Some of these hybrid languages purport to include SQL or SQL-like commands. If they are not relational and are not using the relational algebra in the formation of the SQL portion of their vocabulary, then they are not really using SQL. So, the question arises, who cares? If it looks like SQL and acts like SQL, it must be, as far as anyone cares, SQL. Not necessarily.

SQL queries require a certain database structure, as you have learned, to make them work efficiently. They must contend with the issues of data integrity and a host of multiuser considerations, which we will discuss shortly. Moreover, in order to be usable with distributed data on more than one platform and in more than one database system, they must be SQL under the skin as well as on the surface. Simply using the vocabulary and syntax of SQL does not assure that the language will perform like a real SQL system. In fact, because there is so much going on under the surface to make the commands act like SQL, the performance of a "clone SQL" DBMS may be very poor, indeed.

The tip-off, in most cases, that the hybrid language is using real SQL is that the SQL portion of the language is handled separately from the procedural language. Thus it is necessary for the programmer to embed the SQL commands in the series of procedural commands in one way or another when he or she is writing a database management application.

That does not mean that it is necessary to have separate program segments to handle database manipulation, however. It simply means that the syntax of the language should handle the SQL statements separately from the procedural commands. It is not, it turns out, even necessary for the user or programmer to be aware of the difference.

Throughout this book we will use Gupta Technologies' SQLBase as our example DBMS. This is not an endorsement of SQLBase. Rather, it is an acknowledgment that the product is prevalent in the database management world and that the vocabulary and syntax of its SQL implementation is typical of the industry standard. A bit later in this chapter we will take up the issue of the many SQL implementations available in the market.

However, there is a common type of SQL-like DBMS that contains both a procedural and nonprocedural (SQL) language. These so-called hybrid database management systems are typical of the low-end, relational-like programs that grew from the world of single user PCs. So, as an example of a hybrid DBMS, let's explore dBASE IV SQL both as a procedural and a nonprocedural language. We'll find that dBASE IV SQL is typical of many other, similar systems. Thus, it makes a good example and can further our knowledge of the differences we might encounter in the relational DBMS marketplace.

CHECK YOURSELF

1. What is the difference between a procedural and a nonprocedural language?

2. What is the difference between program flow and data flow?

ANSWERS

1. Procedural languages allow you to create a program made up of procedures including program flow commands. Nonprocedural languages do not allow program flow control.

2. Program flow determines the order in which a program executes commands or statements. Data flow determines how the program manipulates data residing in databases or data tables.

dBASE

dBASE is one of the oldest and most mature of the PC database languages. When we refer to dBASE by itself, we are referring to the language and its extensions. When we use a specific designation, such as dBASE IV or dBASE III Plus, we are referring to a particular Ashton-Tate product that uses the dBASE language. Since the language has evolved over the years, the dBASE reference means the language as it is implemented in dBASE IV, including the SQL portion.

Historically, dBASE was one of the hybrid database languages. It attempted to combine the program flow capabilities of a procedural language with the data flow capabilities of a query language. It succeeded very well on the former, and fell somewhat short on the latter. Even so, for a very long time, dBASE was the only game in town.

As long as dBASE was used only on single PCs in a single-user environment, the deficiencies in its data handling were trivial. When technology advanced to the point where it could be used on networks, in a multiuser environment, it became clear that a better data management mechanism was required. Ashton-Tate selected SQL as that method.

dBASE contains a wealth of procedural commands. The program flow commands are augmented by the use of display-handling commands and functions. Functions are another aspect of virtually all languages. Functions are always considered separately from the command vocabulary and syntax of a language. Thus, you can have a rich set of functions in either a procedural or non-procedural language, since there is no real connection between commands and functions.

While commands instruct the PC's operating system to perform some action, functions are somewhat like miniprograms. When you apply a function to some piece of data, it returns a value. For example, if you have a function that makes each word in a text string start with an uppercase letter, you apply the function to the string and it returns a result. In this case, the result would be the same string, this time with the first letter of each word in uppercase. Functions accept an input, also known as a parameter, and return a result.

SQL systems, even those that do not contain procedural commands, often have extensive sets of functions. The measure, in part, of the usefulness of a database language is the extent of its function set. Functions generally fall into several predictable categories. These categories are indicative of the types of uses to which the functions in them can be put.

Typical function types are mathematical, date, time, and string. Subsets of those categories are financial, scientific, or other specialized mathematical processes. String functions are those that you can use to manipulate strings of text. They include adding or deleting characters, rearranging the characters in a string, and locating the positions of characters in a string.

SQLBase, our model for this book, also has an extremely extensive function set. You can use the SQLBase functions, in most cases, anyway, to add functionality to the SQL statements in the SQLBase vocabulary. Thus, you can extract data indirectly using the result of applying a function to other data. For example, you could subtract days from a current date (a date function) to obtain a range of dates to use as the basis for a database query.

TIP

As you will see later in this book, one of the benefits of using SQL for database queries is that, with a single query statement, you can extract data that would take several procedural statements to locate.

Returning to dBASE for a moment, it provides, outside of its SQL statements, a traditionally dBASE method of manipulating data. However, this set of commands is nowhere near as rich or reliable as the SQL vocabulary. Additionally, the same results obtained with the traditional commands take many lines of code, whereas the SQL statements take only a single statement.

The SQLBase vocabulary is the basic vocabulary specified by ANSI. It also contains several additions or extensions that add to its richness as an SQL implementation. However, you should be aware that many other implementations of SQL contain a different set of SQL extensions (additional, nonstandard statements) from SQLBase.

For our purposes, however, that makes little difference. The syntax of the SQLBase core statements is consistent with most other SQL vocabularies. That means that you, if you have a copy of SQLBase, will be able to try out the exercises in this book. If you have some other SQL DBMS, you should still be able to perform most of the exercises and get similar, if not identical, results as we will with SQLBase.

Procedural and Nonprocedural Languages

CHECK YOURSELF

1. What is a hybrid DBMS?

2. What do functions do?

3. What are some typical types of functions?

ANSWERS

1. A hybrid DBMS is one that contains both procedural and nonprocedural vocabularies.

2. Functions are like miniprograms that accept an input and return a result.

3. Typical function types are mathematical, date, time, and string.

QBE

QBE, or query by example, is an extension of a number of different kinds of query languages. The purpose behind QBE is creating a database query without the need for proficiency in the actual query language. Thus, you could consider QBE to be a query technique as opposed to a query language.

QBE allows you to build up a complex query by answering questions about the query. Your response to the questions allows the program to create a correctly framed database query using the program's query language. For example, a QBE query might begin with a selection of the appropriate database or table. The user is prompted to select from a pick list of available tables or databases. Next, the user is prompted for the column containing the unknown quantity. As an example, you might be using the Customer table of a large sales tracking database. You want to find all of the customers in Ohio. So, the unknown column might be the CUSTOMER column. You would select that from a pick list of all of the columns in the table.

Once you have determined what you want to find, QBE will ask you to select an independent variable. The customer is the dependent variable. That means that its value depends upon the value of some other column. That second column is called the independent variable, because its value is predetermined. It does not depend upon anything. In our example, we want to find customers in Ohio. That means that the independent variable will be located in the STATE column. We want to see customers where the STATE is Ohio. QBE will offer us a pick list of available columns, from which we will select STATE.

Next QBE will want to guide you through defining the known parameters that will determine which customer(s) you select. So it will provide you with a pick list of operators. Perhaps it would offer "equals," "does not equal," "is greater than," "is less than," and "includes." You would pick "equals " because you want all of the customers for whom the STATE column equals "OH." Notice that OH is in quotes. Quotes are used in most query languages when you are searching on a character string instead of a numeric value.

Finally, we need to tell QBE what we expect the contents of the STATE column to equal. In this case, there probably is no pick list. QBE wants us to tell it what to look for. We want all of the customers in Ohio, and we know that states are entered by Postal Service abbreviations, so we enter "OH " (note the quotes). Now QBE will take our answers and formulate a proper query. If the query language is SQL, the final query might be:

SELECT * FROM customers WHERE state = "OH";

The * means that we want to see the entire row (contents of all columns in the row) for each row where the contents of the STATE column is "OH." In a more complex query we might have used more than one table, or displayed only the customer, contact, and phone number. The semicolon at the end of the query is SQL's way of telling you (and the program) that the query is finished. SQL allows many lines in a single query. So, unlike database languages that allow only a single line (in other words, a line terminating in a carriage return), SQL allows several carriage returns. Thus, the carriage return cannot, as in other languages, signify the end of the query. SQL uses the semicolon (;) to do that.

TIP

The point of QBE is that, no matter how complex the query, you can build it up from "examples" without knowing anything about how to frame a proper query or how to use the syntax and commands of the language.

QBE has, in most cases, virtually no impact on the performance of the database. Since it is not a language itself, the query does not execute until you have finished building it up and launching it. Once you launch the query, you are dealing with a correctly framed SQL (or whatever other query language you are using) query. The database program continues as if you had built the query from scratch without the help of QBE. Thus, QBE is nothing more than a tool to help you build correct queries in the appropriate database query language.

SQL

SQL, the topic of this book, is the most popular of query languages. SQL comes in a variety of formats, but the core statements are always the same. Many developers of SQL implementations have added additional statements (called extensions), but the basic commands are consistent from implementation to implementation.

The fact that SQL is consistent from implementation to implementation implies that, no matter what computer it is used on, SQL will always work. Presumably, you could use an SQL database management system (DBMS) on a personal computer to get data out of a different SQL database on a mainframe. That is only partially true. First, let's clear up some semantics. We just referred to "an SQL DBMS " and an "SQL database." The fact is that SQL, being a query language, is not a database. It depends for its success on a relational database that can be queried by the specific SQL DBMS. In SQL-ese, a DBMS is roughly the same as a program in other procedural languages. In fact, as you will learn when we discuss embedded SQL, you can make an SQL DBMS part of a procedural program written in another language. The procedural language controls the nondatabase aspects of the program and the SQL DBMS manages the data with which the rest of the program works.

It turns out that the SQL DBMS, as part of its capabilities, creates the relational database that it is to, eventually, query. If you are reading carefully, you'll begin to see that there is a strong implication that there could be differences in the relational databases created by different SQL DBMS (or implementations). That is an accurate observation. There are slight differences in these relational databases. Thus, for one SQL DBMS to query the relational database created by another SQL DBMS, the querying DBMS must be aware of the differences in the target database.

To understand how SQL database management systems work, we should examine the underlying mechanics of the SQL query process. Once the SQL query is formed, the DBMS must optimize it. That means that the DBMS looks at the query and decides how it will execute the various statements, clauses, and predicates that make it up. In other words, the DBMS decides the best order to execute the query's commands. To do that, the query "engine" (the underlying SQL program code written by the developers of whatever SQL package you are using) must understand the database format, file format, indexes, if any, and other factors that affect its ability to locate a particular record in the table.

Once it has optimized the query, the DBMS starts looking for the appropriate tables and locating the correct rows in them. As it locates a row whose columns meet the search criteria, it needs to know what to display. Finally, the DBMS displays its results and moves on to find the next appropriate row. If the target table has an unfamiliar format, it will often return nothing or, at least, an erroneous result. However, if the DBMS has been able to optimize the query for more than one table format, it can search for data in more than one type of relational database. You should also understand that the differences in data storage format are, usually, greater than the differences in table or database format.

The differences in data storage format often have more to do with the platform on which they reside than in differences in relational database philosophy. What that means is that file format on an IBM mainframe, for example, is far different from the file format on a personal computer. Thus, if we have an SQL program on a PC that wants to query a relational database on a mainframe, we must insure that our PC program can understand the file and database format on the mainframe.

Most distributed database programs using SQL accomplish this by means of translators. Translators accept the query from the querying system in its own format and reoptimize it for the target format. The target system then returns the results to the translator, which delivers the results in the querying program's format. The outcome is that the querying program has full use of the target tables as if they were in the program's own format. This process allows distributed database management between different platforms and programs as long as all systems use the same SQL statement set.

That is, unfortunately, the next potential pitfall. As we said, not all SQL DBMS are the same. True, they contain the same core set of statements. But what if we have a DBMS that supports extensions that the target system does not? How will the target system's translator reoptimize the query? The short answer is that it won't.

Procedural and Nonprocedural Languages

Taking the issue no further than this, the target system will "choke" on the unknown query.

The solution is that the developers of the querying system, not the target system, provide the translator. The translator contains a procedure for filtering unknown queries so that they are optimized into the statement set of the target system. If the target system supports statements that the querying system does not, those statements simply are not used. The result is that some of the available functionality of the target system will be lost.

For our purposes, we will stick fairly close to the statement set found in the core implementation of SQL. This is the part of the language that is reasonably consistent from implementation to implementation. Our example, as we have said, is Gupta Technologies' SQLBase. With very few exceptions you can use our examples with most SQL programs and get similar results.

CHECK YOURSELF

1. What is QBE?

2. What is the difference between QBE and SQL?

3. What is the benefit of SQL?

ANSWERS

1. QBE is query by example. The user is asked to fill in some blanks regarding the nature of the query and the QBE system forms the query.

2. QBE forms the query based upon the information supplied by the user, usually in English instead of a database language. SQL requires that the user be familiar with the SQL language and can form the database query from scratch.

3. SQL provides a consistent query language, which contains a few core commands that can be used in data manipulation statements replacing the many lines of code required by procedural languages to accomplish the same task. It is also reasonably simple to use and learn and has very powerful data manipulation capabilities.

DB2—Why Is It Important?

In the early days of large mainframe computers, one of the most important applications was database management. If you think about it, you'll see that, even in today's world of "downsizing," most business applications have some need for databases of information. So, today, as it was in the earlier days of computing, database management remains the mainstay of business applications.

However, in those earlier times, there was a need that was not yet met. That need was for a robust, multiuser database language. Even before the language could be developed, though, there was the need for the database structure. With the evolution of the relational model, SQL became the generalized query language of choice to go along with it.

IBM, needing to adapt the relational model and SQL to a useful product that worked on an IBM platform, created two general purpose SQL products that are in use today. Of the two, SQL/DS and DB2, DB2 is the most popular. In fact, DB2 has almost become a de facto standard for large SQL database implementations. Thus, it has become important that serious PC relational databases be able to exchange data with a DB2 database.

Not long after that, Oracle Corporation developed a similar product for use on Digital Equipment Corporation VAXes. Oracle has evolved their product, Oracle Server, into a system that can operate on PCs running UNIX or OS/2 and VAXes. It can, of course, exchange data with IBM DB2 databases. SQLBase, our model DBMS, also communicates directly with DB2 and Oracle databases as well as Microsoft Corporation's SQL Server product. In fact, SQLBase can be used as the hub of a distributed SQL DBMS,

Procedural and Nonprocedural Languages

TIP

DB2 has become the baseline SQL DBMS with which all other systems seek to connect. That means that not only does the DBMS need to maintain a language syntax and database structure consistent with DB2, it must also have a method of translating queries so that the IBM mainframe running DB2 can make some sense of them.

exchanging data with a wide variety of database backends (the DB2, Oracle, SQL Server, SQLBase, and other databases) and frontends (the programs that interact directly with the user at the PC and allow manipulation of the database data).

As we pointed out earlier, not all DBMSs, even SQL DBMSs, are the same, even though they may appear so. In the case of using a variety of different platforms and programs in a mixed database environment (called a heterogeneous database system), it is useful if everything conforms to a common standard. Over the years the ANSI committee on SQL has put together a standard for the language and the way it interacts with DBMS.

That standard is very similar to the IBM SQL implementation found in DB2. Thus, systems that meet the ANSI SQL standard can usually, with some help on the platform and operating system side, exchange data with other, dissimilar systems. Without the marketing power of IBM behind DB2, it is very likely that our current versions of SQL would look somewhat different than they do.

SQL on PCs

Today, SQL has come in full flower to the smallest of computing platforms, personal computers. SQL demonstrates its greatest strength as a data manipulation language in a multiuser environment, so it was only natural that its popularity would be somewhat limited until good multiuser solutions for PCs evolved. In the UNIX and OS/2 worlds, SQL database management systems have been popular for some time. However, because of the single user nature of DOS on PCs, there was little incentive to develop SQL products.

The result has been that single user database systems, called single file systems, proliferated in the early years of PCs. It wasn't long, however, before PC DBMS developers realized that they needed to work with more than one table at a time. They needed to be able to "relate" data in one table to data in another table and develop a composite table containing information from both, connected in some meaningful way. Thus the relational-like PC database management systems, like dBASE, came onto the PC scene.

It was usually the case that the developers of these systems viewed their systems almost as programming languages. They felt that users wanted to be able to develop database applications from their products. Thus, the developers needed a language that contained both procedural and nonprocedural aspects. For the user who wished to make casual or ad hoc queries of the database, there were nonprocedural methods for doing so. If the user wished to build an application that used the database management capabilities of the program to perform repetitive tasks, that was OK too. However, very little about most database management systems in the early days of PCs looked anything like SQL (with the exception of one early database system called Condor, now defunct).

And, certainly, the need for a real relational data structure wasn't felt until multiuser systems became a reality for PCs. What happened at that point was that PC databases took two distinct directions that have, unfortunately, blurred over time. One direction was the revamping of single user products into kludges that could allow users in a multiuser PC (local area network, or LAN) environment to have some of the benefits of real multiuser systems.

The second direction, followed by such developers as Oracle, Gupta, and Microsoft, was to build, from scratch, a true multiuser DBMS that could operate in a distributed LAN environment. Naturally, these developers surveyed the large DBMS market and found that corporate users (the ones most likely to need a multiuser DBMS) were using the relational model and SQL. These forward-looking developers created their products using the same relational model and SQL. As LANs have matured, the popularity of SQL DBMS on PCs has also matured.

The result is that corporate users can now implement complex, powerful, robust database applications using SQL products that can coexist in a heterogeneous environment. There are, today, almost as many application development tools available for the PC SQL leaders as there are for mainframe systems. The next few sections of this chapter will discuss the nature of three different ways to implement SQL in a PC database application.

Procedural and Nonprocedural Languages

CHECK YOURSELF

1. What is DB2 and why is it important?

2. What are the two directions taken by PC database developers and why are they important?

ANSWERS

1. DB2 is one of two SQL DBMS implementations by IBM. It is the most popular and, therefore, the one most other systems need to be able to connect with.

2. PC database developers chose either to modify existing single user products for LAN use or to build true multi-user database management systems. Those that chose the latter were able to use SQL and the relational model to achieve the potential for cross-platform connectivity and data sharing.

Interactive SQL

By far the most familiar of SQL implementations is interactive SQL. Interactive SQL simply means that the user formulates the SQL statement from some sort of prompt or using a text editor. The SQL that we will explore throughout this book is interactive SQL. That is, we will use SQLBase's built-in editor, SQLTalk, to write real SQL queries and build our SQL databases. Almost every type of SQL system allows, at some level, interactive SQL.

There are advantages and disadvantages to interactively forming SQL statements. First, you need to know the SQL syntax in order to build an effective statement. That's what this book is all about. Second, the SQL language is an often frustrating combination of simplicity and complexity. It is simple in that there are very few actual commands or, in SQL-ese, statements. It is complex in that those few statements have a wide variety of uses.

SQL statements, as you will learn in much more detail later, are usually many lines long. Often, those lines have only a few words in them, but how you write those words can make a tremendous difference in your results. Using SQL is not programming, but it has many of the elements of programming. For example, you will need to think out precisely what you want the query to do before you type it on your screen. Like a programming language, SQL does exactly what you tell it to do in exactly the order you tell SQL to do it.

The SQL syntax is very precise and must be followed exactly. SQL is not a forgiving language. When you complete an entire statement, you need a method to tell your computer that you have finished and it can execute the statement. In most database languages, that means that you simply hit the carriage return. That won't work with SQL, though. Since it has several lines in each statement, there are often several carriage returns. So SQL has the convention that you end every statement with a semicolon (;). That is the PC's cue to process the statement.

TIP

One of the most common syntax errors when using interactive SQL is ignoring the semicolon at the end of the statement. Since the statement can't execute without it, you'll get some rather strange error messages, depending upon the SQL program you are using. Don't forget the semicolon!

We'll use interactive SQL throughout this book, forming our statements with SQLTalk. As we formulate our statements and perform various exercises, we'll leave out that portion of the example that relates specifically to SQLTalk. Since you may be forming your practice statements on a different system, you'll need to know how to access your system's SQL editor.

Embedded SQL

When we include SQL statements in a program that is otherwise written in a procedural language, we say the SQL portion is embedded in the procedural portion. For example, we may be writing a database application in C or Cobol or, in fact, just about any other language. The language that we are using has the advantage of being able to do just about anything that we want it to except handle data.

These procedural programming languages are very good at creating screen displays, allowing detailed and complex program flow control, and lots of other things that programming languages are supposed to do. But they are very weak at manipulating data. Furthermore, you couldn't build a consistent database management system if every programmer built the database portion a different way. So programmers embed the SQL statements in their procedural program.

That sounds simple. However, unless there is some mechanism for the program compiler to recognize the SQL commands, there will be no way to use the SQL. So there are a couple of methods for embedding SQL in a procedural program. Which of these you use depends upon the implementation of the programming language. The simple implementation is to have a set of SQL commands as part of the programming language that you can use in your application. This is called invisible SQL. By using the SQL commands as part of the application, you simply need to enter the statement exactly as you would interactively. The difference is that you are including it in your program instead of using it "live " from an SQL editor prompt. In the case of dBASE IV SQL, for example, you simply create a special program file that dBASE IV recognizes as containing both dBASE commands and SQL statements.

The dBASE IV implementation of SQL is contained within the dBASE IV language. There are no outside programs, libraries, or utilities to use. You include the appropriate SQL command in your program code. You use dBASE IV SQL statements when you want the program to access a data table. Once you have the desired results, your application can continue and execute using the data in whatever way you intended when you wrote the application.

The benefit is that embedded SQL is just about as fast to do its work as any set of commands in the program. You, as a programmer, don't have to deal with the complexities of attaching SQL to your program externally. And the application performs better and is more seamless (the data handling is less obvious to the user) than with just about any other method.

However, there are potentially some drawbacks. The SQL portion of the program needs to be optimized for the SQL query. Often programming languages that have invisible SQL as part of their language syntax don't fully optimize the query into a "real " SQL statement (in other words, the underlying program code to execute the statement you wrote). The result is that such languages, and dBASE is one of them, have difficulty communicating with other SQL databases.

The second approach, precompiled SQL, works somewhat the opposite from invisible SQL. Precompiled SQL is a form of embedded SQL that works from outside the source language (C, Fortran, Cobol, etc.). The idea behind precompiled SQL is that you embed the SQL capability into the source language from some outside source. That outside source must have an application programming interface (API) for the source language. You must precompile the SQL portion of the program and add it to the source language program before you compile the source language code.

The result is that performance is quite good, you have some flexibility in your use of source languages, and you can stick close to an SQL implementation that meets standards. The application program executes the precompiled SQL statements essentially as if they were part of the source language program. You have allowed the source language to do what it does best: control the program. And you have used SQL to do what it was made to do: manipulate data. The SQL part of the program passes its data to the source language program by means of parameters. The source language program uses special commands, such as EXEC, to tell the SQL program that it needs its services.

In this book we won't spend much more time with embedded SQL, since we are not particularly concerned with building complex source language programs with SQL data-handling capability (in Chapter 9 we will take the subject up in somewhat more detail, albeit from a generic point of view). However, it is good to understand, at least on an elementary level for the moment, how SQL can be used in procedural language applications. Recognizing that you can embed SQL in a source language program explains how SQL—a nonprocedural query language—can be used in an application to simplify repetitive database management tasks.

Procedural and Nonprocedural Languages

CHECK YOURSELF

1. What is the difference between interactive and embedded SQL?

2. How can you embed SQL in a procedural language application?

ANSWERS

1. Interactive SQL requires that the user enter the SQL statement using a query editor from a prompt. Embedded SQL is part of a database management application. The user never sees the actual statement.

2. You can embed SQL in a procedural program by using invisible SQL if the procedural language has its own SQL. dBASE IV is an example. You can also embed SQL in a procedural program if the SQL implementation you are using has an API and allows you to precompile the SQL queries.

Multiuser Solutions

Multiuser databases are the lifeblood of most large DBMS applications. So, it follows that any competent DBMS should perform well in a multiuser environment. We mentioned earlier that it was the growth of local area networks that really brought SQL and the relational model into wider use on PCs. Now, let's explore some of the implications of a multiuser database management system.

We'll start by defining a bit more clearly what we mean by a multiuser environment. There are two types of multiuser environments that we must consider. It should be obvious that one of the requirements for such an environment is that there be more than one user trying to access data on the database at the same time. So we'll take that as a given. However, depending upon the architecture of the system on which the DBMS resides, those users might be accessing the data in very different ways.

The first way, typical of mainframe computers, uses the centralized computing model where all of the processing takes place at a central computer. The user sits at a terminal that is, really, little more than a window into the mainframe. The terminal, beyond such mundane tasks as screen formatting, does no data processing or manipulation. All of that is done by the central computer. This is called master-slave architecture because the computer is the master, which does the work and displays the results to the terminal, or slave. The second type of multiuser environment, typical of PC LANs, is called client-server computing. The simple explanation is that both the host and the user's PC participate in the actual data processing. The host, usually called a database server, handles the data manipulation under instructions from the remote workstation (called the client). The client executes the application in its memory. When the client requires data, the client instructs the database server to perform an SQL command or statement and deliver the results to the client.

The database server performs the query, relieving the client of the task, and delivers only the data meeting the request to the workstation. The client does its job, the server does its, and the traffic over the network is minimized because only the requested data returns to the client. In such an environment there can be many database servers and many clients. The clients can, under the right conditions, access data from multiple servers. That architecture is further defined as distributed database management. Client-server architecture has proven to be the most efficient way to manage large amounts of data in an SQL environment.

Multiuser Solutions

TIP

When a client must have access to data on several servers that are of different types, such as mainframes, PCs, and minicomputers, we say that the environment is heterogeneous. That means that there are several different types of hardware platforms and operating systems in the DBMS.

Obviously, when we operate in these various, and different, multiuser environments, we have requirements for controlling access. In Chapter 1 we introduced you to two of those requirements: concurrency control and data integrity. SQL provides us with some tools for enforcing those requirements in a multiuser DBMS.

File and Record Locking

There are two fundamental premises of multiuser database management. The first is that two users can't be allowed to change a database record at the same time without informing each other of their intentions. The second is that when multiple tables are involved in an update, the update must be reversible until all the tables have been safely and correctly changed. SQL handles the first with a type of file and record locking. It allows the user to handle the second through transaction processing. Let's take first things first.

There are two times when we need to lock a user out of a record or table. The first is when another user is doing an update to a record. The second is when a batch update is being done to the entire database or a table in it. SQL handles the first by locking the record while the first user is writing a change to it. It handles the second by locking the entire table being updated. An example of a table update is adding or deleting a record or changing indexing. The object of locking out users is to prevent the loss of concurrency control (see Chapter 1). Said another way, preserving concurrency control allows the maximum number of users to access the same data without interfering with each other or corrupting the data.

Because you build SQL statements to perform a complete task (such as changing a record or updating a table), the actual duration of use of a record or file lock is quite brief. Unlike procedural programs, which must execute a complex series of commands, SQL statements include all of the information the DBMS needs to complete a single procedure. Thus the program (if you are embedding SQL in an application) doesn't need to execute a series of commands to protect data since SQL handles that task.

If you are using SQL interactively, instead of issuing a series of commands that could lock a record while you (slowly, perhaps) type out the commands, you simply enter the statement into the SQL editor and execute. Nothing is happening to the data as you type. In fact, there is no action at all until you hit the <Enter> key after typing the final semicolon. Then the execution depends only on the speed of your computer and the efficiency of your SQL command or statement.

Transaction Processing

SQL provides concurrency control through file and record locking without involving the user and also provides database integrity by supplying the tools for the user to make sure that updates are complete before engraving them in stone. Those tools are used for a special type of procedure called transaction processing. The tools are the COMMIT and ROLLBACK statements.

We won't go into too much detail about transaction processing, since you must be embedding SQL in an application to use it. However, in Chapter 9 we will discuss the use of COMMIT and ROLLBACK in a bit more detail. For the moment, here is how the technique of transaction processing can help preserve data integrity.

The reason that you must embed SQL into a procedural application is that the task of updating several tables must be accomplished one table at a time. Each update requires a separate SQL statement. Not until all of the statements have executed have you updated all of the required tables. If you interrupt the process in the middle, some tables will be updated while others won't. The result is similar to your checkbook being out of balance. Nothing matches anymore.

When you use transaction processing to update several tables, you write a program that performs the updates one at a time, but considers all of them together as a single transaction. The program does not consider the transaction complete until all of the updates have been performed successfully. When the updates are complete and correct, you issue a COMMIT statement, which makes the updates permanent.

If, for some reason, the transaction, meaning all of the included updates, does not complete successfully, you issue a ROLLBACK. The ROLLBACK returns all of the tables involved in the transaction to the state they were in just prior to its commencement. The mechanism for defining an incomplete transaction could be a timeout (the transaction does not complete after a preprogrammed period of time), an interruption (the system crashes before the transaction completes), or any other parameter that the programmer wishes to use as an event to initiate a ROLLBACK.

QUICK SUMMARY

Here are some of the important points in this chapter. The word or phrase in bold lists a relational database feature. That feature's definition and its benefit to you follows.

Procedural languages These are programming languages that you can use to write a program for automating a repetitive task. For a language to be considered procedural it must provide both data flow and program flow control. In other words, it must allow you to define a series of steps that the program must execute and save those steps for future use when you execute the program.

Nonprocedural languages These languages do not have the capability of program flow control. You cannot program a series of steps for the language to execute on its own. An example of a nonprocedural language is a query language such as SQL. Each command in such a language must be executed one at a time manually under the control of the user.

SQL-like language limitations Many PC database programs, such as dBASE IV, use a form of SQL. The statements closely follow the SQL standard, but those programs often do not translate the statements in such a way as to be compatible with other standard SQL databases.

QBE as a form of SQL QBE, query by example, allows users to build SQL queries without a formal knowledge of the language. By responding to questions, the user provides the QBE system information it uses to formulate a correct SQL query.

The importance of DB2 DB2, an IBM implementation of SQL, generally provided the de facto standard from which ANSI SQL grew. Virtually every serious SQL DBMS should be able to exchange data with a DB2 database.

The difference between interactive and embedded SQL Interactive SQL is SQL that the user must use, a statement at a time, from within an SQL editor or from a screen prompt. Embedded SQL is SQL that executes from within a procedural language application.

Some important multiuser considerations Multiuser DBMS must be able to preserve data integrity and concurrency control.

SQL manages concurrency control through file and record locking. It provides COMMIT and ROLLBACK as tools for transaction processing when building applications with embedded SQL.

PRACTICE WHAT YOU'VE LEARNED

1. Compare procedural and nonprocedural languages and give examples of each.

2. Describe QBE and tell how it is used for SQL.

3. Contrast interactive and embedded SQL.

4. Describe the two types of embedded SQL and give examples of each.

5. What are the advantages of the two types of embedded SQL? The disadvantages?

6. Describe two architectures for a multiuser DBMS.

7. Briefly describe two important requirements of a multiuser DBMS.

ANSWERS

1. Procedural languages are those that allow you to program a series of steps that the program executes sequentially. Procedural languages must be capable of providing program flow control. dBASE, C, Fortran, Cobol, and similar languages are procedural. Nonprocedural languages do not allow you to program steps and do not provide any type of program flow control. Typical nonprocedural languages are query languages such as SQL.

2. QBE, query by example, is a front-end technique for providing the user with a way to formulate a query without being familiar with the actual query language. The user fills in blanks that describe the information desired and its location (i.e., the name of the database). From the user's responses the QBE builds a correct query and returns the information to the user. QBE is often used with SQL programs to provide

an easy way for users unfamiliar with SQL to query an SQL database.

3. Interactive SQL requires that the user enter each command or statement, one at a time, using an SQL editor. Embedded SQL is a variety of SQL that allows users to build a program, using a procedural language, and use SQL statements within the program for manipulating data in a relational database.

4. Embedded SQL can be either invisible, as in dBASE IV, or precompiled, as in SQLBase. Invisible SQL is actually part of the DBMS program language. That language usually contains a set of procedural commands to provide program flow control, and a set of SQL commands to provide data manipulation. The SQL commands are included directly in the procedures programmed by the user into a database application. Precompiled SQL is external to the procedural language and must be prepared using a precompiler for use in the application. The SQL statement usually is called from within the procedural language code using commands such as EXEC.

5. Invisible SQL is easier to use than precompiled SQL in a database application because it is part of the programming language's command set. However, it may not be, in the underlying code, a true implementation of SQL. Pre-compiled SQL is more difficult to use—it usually requires a programmer expert in the use of the procedural host language—but provides better performance and SQL compatibility with other systems to which the application may wish to connect.

6. A multiuser DBMS may be master-slave or client-server. Master-slave systems use the centralized computing model wherein all of the actual computing is done on a central computer such as a mainframe. The client-server architecture allows computing to be divided between workstations and centralized computers as on PC LANs. The client (user PC workstation) runs the application and issues requests for data to the database server. The server executes the

request and returns the data to the client application for further processing.

7. A multiuser DBMS must provide for concurrency control and data integrity. It supports concurrency control with file and record locking. It provides COMMIT and ROLLBACK for use in embedded SQL applications using transaction processing to insure data integrity.

The SQL
Structure

We've explored the basics of relational database management systems and database query techniques. These first two chapters introduced you to some database management theory in general and, specifically, prepared you to dig deeper into SQL. In this chapter we'll continue with the basics. This time, however, we'll focus on SQL in particular and discuss the structure of an SQL database management system. In this chapter you will learn:

▲ The structure of an SQL database

▲ How SQL uses a data dictionary to track data tables

▲ What tables are and their relationship to databases

▲ How SQL uses indexes and views

▲ The types of data in an SQL database

The SQL Database

With many types of database management systems, when we speak of databases we mean a single file of data. We may, in some cases, include indexes, either directly or by inference. In an SQL DBMS, however, the term database has a somewhat different meaning. If you'll recall, in Chapter 1 we discussed the relational model. Many relational-like database management systems attempt to achieve a semblance of relationality by building commands that relate two or more databases. In other words, they are treating individual database files as if they were relational.

Let's try to simplify this a bit. Consider, for a moment, that you have two separate and unrelated database files. They have absolutely nothing in common except that each has a single field that is identical. In other words, the field has exactly the same field definition, field name, and data. Thus, we could build a command that allowed us to connect these two dissimilar files based solely upon their common field. This is a sort of pseudorelationality. It is the type of relationship you can create with programs like dBASE III Plus and (excluding its SQL capability) dBASE IV.

However, the lack of a true relationship (as defined using Codd's rules and relational algebra) impedes us somewhat in areas of multiuser systems and large database management systems. We find that there are limitations on how many of these dissimilar databases we can relate. We find that one to many, many to one, and many to many relationships are, often, convoluted and difficult to operate with. In SQL, however, we have a better way of arranging data.

SQL databases are, actually, collections of tables of data. These tables contain the various data sets that we want to work with for a particular application. In other words, if, for example, we wanted to build an accounting application, we might set up an accounting database. That database might consist of an accounts receivable table and an accounts payable table, as well as tables for customers, suppliers, purchase orders, and all of the other separate tables you would expect in such an application.

In SQL we refer to the database and its components as objects. SQL objects include the database itself, the tables that make up the database, indexes for the tables, and views that represent data from several tables. The use of objects is an ideal way to manage data because it does not demand that you predefine the relationships between parts of the database.

For example, in other types of databases (other than relational) you must define a pointer that indicates the record that contains the data you want. By setting up rules for moving the pointer, you locate your data. These rules are part of the query process, but they have to be predefined. SQL and relational databases use a somewhat different approach.

Instead of storing data as pointers, which we then relate using predefined procedures, SQL allows you to use any value in a database object to relate two or more tables. You select those values and the relations you wish to use to locate data at the time of creating the query.

One final word about the benefits of the relational model in general and SQL in particular is in order here. Earlier in this book we referred to optimizing SQL queries. Here's a bit more on what that means. In most SQL DBMS, certainly in SQLBase, optimization performs the following. When you execute an SQL statement, you are, actually, telling the DBMS to perform some operation on data. You may be adding a row or column, retrieving data from a single table, or relating two or more tables to retrieve data. The SQL DBMS looks at your query and decides how to best perform your task. It may decide to use an index, use a table alone, or use both. You never need to specify the use of an index as with other database programs. SQL does all that for you. The process by which SQL breaks down your command and decides how to go about performing it is called optimizing.

Having said that, we do not mean to imply that the creation of indexes should always be left to the DBMS. Good DBMS design dictates that you specify indexes to the extent that is practical and consistent with the way you expect the application to be used. However, unlike other types of database management systems, SQL will, if the situation dictates, create an index for you. These indexes are temporary ones, created by the optimizer. As with anything the optimizer does based upon its own decisions, there is

The SQL Database

a price to pay in terms of performance. Thus, for best performance, you, as a DBMS designer, should anticipate when the use of an index is appropriate and create it whenever possible.

TIP

Whenever possible, anticipate the need for indexes in your DBMS application and create them yourself. The DBMS can do that for you, but you will sacrifice performance because it takes time for the optimizer to decide that it needs another index and create it.

The Data Dictionary

We keep track of the tables and their indexes using a special table or set of tables called a data dictionary or, sometimes, a catalog. The data dictionary is a "table of tables." It contains the database structure, the structure of each of the tables in the database, all of the indexes and key fields, as well as other pertinent information about the database. The database itself may usually be thought of as little more than a directory having the database name that contains all of the tables, indexes, views and other pieces that make up the whole database. In fact, some SQL database management systems actually arrange their databases in exactly that manner.

In SQLBase, the data dictionary is called the System Catalog. The catalog is maintained by the DBMS automatically. You do not have to be concerned with it at all other than to know that it exists and what its purposes are. However, if you need information about the database, you can query the catalog just like any other table in the database. When you make a change to one of the tables in the database, the change is reflected automatically in the catalog.

SQLBase uses ten tables for its system catalog, or data dictionary, which contain information similar to that maintained by other SQL data dictionaries. The tables and their purposes are as follows:

SYSCOLAUTH—The users and their column update privileges
SYSCOLUMNS—The columns in the database
SYSCOMMANDS—The commands stored in the database
SYSINDEXES—All of the indexes in the database

SYSKEYS—All of the columns in the indexes
SYSSYNONYMS—All the synonyms of the tables and views
SYSTABAUTH—The users and their table privileges
SYSTABLES—The tables and views in the database
SYSUSERAUTH—The users and their database level privileges
SYSVIEWS—The views in the database. Each database will
  have its own unique data dictionary.

**The SQL
Database**

CHECK YOURSELF

1. In SQL terms, what is a database?

2. What does the data dictionary or system catalog do?

3. In terms of database structure, what is a key advantage of the relational database?

ANSWERS

1. A database is a collection of tables, indexes, and views.

2. The data dictionary contains tables of information about the database, its tables, indexes, and views. It is how the SQL database retains information about the files, users, and data that make it up.

3. The relational database does not require that you predefine pointers to establish data relationships. You can define relationships "on the fly" as you create SQL queries.

Tables

We said earlier that SQL·uses tables to organize data. These tables may be actual individual files or they may be included in a larger database file. That varies from DBMS program to program. Regardless of the physical organization of the tables, each table is unique and has its own name. When you want to retrieve data from a table you refer to it by name. Prior to accessing a data table, of course, you must open the database that contains it. Generally, the SQL command for opening a database is START.

TIP

Different implementations of SQL often use different commands from those in the so-called "core commands" set up by ANSI. The commands, however, must do the same thing. START is a good example of this. In SQLBase the equivalent command is CONNECT.

Tables in SQL look like the familiar spreadsheets you have seen in programs like Lotus 1-2-3. They consist of rows and columns. We do not refer to the intersection of these rows and columns as cells (as in a spreadsheet), however. To aid you in relating the tabular SQL structure to the simpler databases with which you may be familiar, we'll reiterate some terms we introduced in an earlier chapter. The table's rows are similar to records in nonrelational databases. The columns are the individual fields. We may think of the intersection of the rows and columns as data elements.

There are a few rules we alluded to earlier, as well. For example, rows in a table should be unique. That means that you would not place the exact same data in more than one row of a particular table. In order to avoid this, you will need to plan your table structure carefully.

For example, if it is conceivable that you could, with the data you anticipate, have two duplicate rows, then you should make a provision for showing a difference between the two. There are many ways to do this. You could add a column for sequence numbers. Each new entry would then get a new and unique sequence number. You could time stamp the entries with a column for time. Each row, then, would have a unique time stamp that would differentiate it from all other rows, even though the rest of the data may be identical with that in another row. The data in such a column (the one that makes the row unique) can then be used as a primary key.

The term primary key has been introduced to you previously. Here, then, is a more detailed explanation of it. You use primary keys to connect two or more tables together. In order for a column to be a primary key, the values in it must be unique to each row. In other words, you cannot have more than one row whose data element has the same value in the column that you choose as the primary key.

When you have two or more tables, each containing the same column and the same data elements, you can combine or join those tables based upon the data element values in the primary key. The identical columns and data in the subsequent tables are called foreign keys. Here, however, is a distinction that may seem a bit tricky. We just said that we were dealing with identical columns and data elements.

That is not strictly true. It is possible that one or the other table may have data elements in its key column (primary key in the main table and foreign keys in others) that are not identical from table to table. When that is the case, only those rows where the data elements match exactly will be used in a join. However, the columns themselves must be identical and they must be unique within their tables.

When we have primary, or parent keys that exactly match foreign keys, we have referential integrity. It is possible to have a foreign key refer back to a primary or parent key in its own table. This is a sort of circular reference and it is not without the potential for problems. The foreign key, in this case, need not be unique. In the case that it is not unique it would, of course, be possible to get repeat values of the foreign key for the unique values of the primary key.

There are actually two ways of dealing with referential integrity. Depending upon the DBMS, referential integrity may be enforced by the underlying structure of the database management system (as it is in later versions of SQLBase) or it may need to be enforced by the external application (the one you, as database management application developer, write). The difference is that in DBMS enforced referential integrity, the DBMS knows its keys. In application enforced referential integrity, the DBMS does not. In that case, it is up to you to insure that referential integrity is maintained.

For example, let us imagine a table with a primary key of zip code and a foreign key of state. We are, perhaps, setting up a sales force wherein there will be but one salesperson in any given zip code. Thus, the zip code column would contain unique values; with only one salesperson per zip code, each zip code could appear only once in the table.

But, of course, there would be many times that zip codes could refer to the same state. Therefore, using the primary key to refer back to the foreign key in the same table, we would see the same data element (the state) appear multiple times for many different incidences of the primary key (the zip codes). If we restrain the foreign key to referencing a specified table, we are enforcing a referential constraint.

We also can use keys to join tables. We can, therefore, create a view (which we will discuss shortly) based upon selected columns from all of the joined tables. Only the rows that meet the criteria of our query will be included in the new table (the view).

SQL and the Index

You have learned that SQL does not use indexes in the same way that other database management systems do. Now we'll discuss why this is so and what it means. In most other types of database management systems, an index is a physical file that contains the order of records in a database based upon a particular key. Here, the term "key" takes on a somewhat different meaning. In general terms, regardless of the database type, a key is a key. However, when we examine the fine points of the issue, we find that such is not quite the case.

Compared to true relational databases, there are far fewer restrictions placed on the selection of keys, or key fields, in other types of databases. For example, you can usually have key fields whose data is not unique. The problem with that is that you will then need a secondary key in order to insure data integrity. The secondary key is the one that the database will look to in case it finds two records with the same value in the key field. As you might guess, this is a bit of a kludge. Of course, a good database designer will realize that he or she puts data integrity at risk by designing a data structure that allows duplicate keys and will avoid the practice.

Index files in databases other than relational ones, therefore, list the record numbers in the order inferred from the contents of the key field. When you query such a database, it checks the index file and places the record pointer at the database record containing the value of the key field from the index. Let's examine that process.

First, you must have determined that, when a user makes a query, the query will be based upon the contents of a particular field. Then you must insure that you have created an index for that key field. The program must then realize that the query is based upon the database and the appropriate index, go to that index, and pick up a record number. Finally, the database application will go to the database and set the record pointer at the record number indicated by the index. If, for some reason, the index has been corrupted or has not been properly updated, the record pointer will end up at the wrong record.

Remember that the pointer goes to a record number based upon instructions from the index. It has no knowledge of the contents of the record. All it knows is that the index claimed that record number such-and-so contained the desired data. And off it goes, merrily seeking that record. If the index is wrong, that's too bad. The pointer has obeyed its instructions.

A relational database, though, doesn't have these problems. Theoretically, every table can be indexed on every column. When you form a query, the SQL optimizer decides if the value(s) you seek would be most easily located by viewing one or more columns as keys and indexing on them or simply reading the table. It may decide that a combination of the two would be most effective. The point is that a relational SQL database management system is aware of the data in its tables. When it searches for values as the result of a query, it takes the actual data elements, as well as possible keys, into account. The process, while not as fast, is certain. There is another benefit. You don't have to decide in advance what the keys should be. You can include that information as you form your SQL query and let the query optimizer do the rest. However, remember that the price you pay for your laziness is performance.

The indexes, once they have been defined in SQLBase are maintained, along with the keys, by the system. Most SQL DBMS work the same way. The specifics, of course, differ from system to system. But, in general, the process is similar. The data dictionary or catalog keeps track of the indexes and the keys. In SQLBase, there are two tables in the catalog that track these two important issues.

The SYSINDEXES table contains one row for each index including the indexes on the tables in the catalog. That means that every time SQLBase builds an index, it is recorded in the catalog. Next, the SYSKEYS table in the catalog contains a row for each column in an index. Taken with the SYSCOLUMNS table in the catalog, which contains a row for every column in every table in the database, that allows indexing on any column as a key in any table in the database on a roughly ad hoc basis.

SQL indexes have some major benefits to users. First, they dramatically improve performance. Since the system does not have to search every column of every row in every table to find the data requested in a query, access to the desired data is quite speedy. Also, when indexing is done correctly, maintaining integrity and uniqueness of keys, data integrity, and consistency is preserved. Since indexing in SQL can be maintained by the database system, and there is no specific requirement to designate indexes in advance, there is far less chance of an index not matching actual data in a table. Still, as we have emphasized, whenever possible, you should create the appropriate indexes and not leave the chore to the optimizer.

CHECK YOURSELF

1. What is the requirement for a primary key?

2. How do SQL indexes differ from indexes in nonrelational or relational-like databases?

3. What are some of the benefits to indexing?

ANSWERS

1. The primary key must be a column whose data elements are unique.

2. SQL indexes do not require that you predefine the index and the data elements that make it up. SQL sets up the index automatically when you form your query.

3. Indexes improve performance and insure uniqueness and data integrity.

Views

A view is, really, not a physical table. It is, instead, a virtual table made up of rows and columns that you select using an SQL query. However, so that you can repeat the view, SQL stores a definition of it in the data dictionary. Thus you can have a view that acts, for all intents and purposes, like a physical table of data.

There are a couple of kinds of views. One is a subset of a single table. You might use that kind of view when you want to extract data from a table, but you don't want all of the table. You can build a query to extract the data you want each time you want to see it. However, it is often easier to create a view and then look at all the data in the view. Another use for this type of view is that it allows you to view the same data in different ways. Since you can treat the view as if it were a physical table, you always have the most current data in your view, regardless of how you choose to view it.

Another reason, often the most important one, for using this type of view is maintaining the security of information in the table. By limiting the columns a user can see, sensitive data can be hidden from view. For example, you might choose to withhold the salary column from a view of a payroll table for certain groups of users.

The second kind of view is created as the result of a join. This is the most common use for a view. Joins are often the result of rather complex SQL queries. Thus, if you want to make the query process easier for users, you might choose to create a view from the query and, subsequently, use the view instead of the complex query.

Views differ from physical tables in that they actually don't exist. What does exist is the definition of the view. Therefore, when you query a view (which you can, just as if it were a table), you are actually querying a set of instructions. SQL uses those instructions to build a virtual table in your PC's memory and then it extracts the data in the same way it would in a physical table. If your PC runs out of memory, SQL treats the view in exactly the same way it would a physical table under the same circumstances: it simply creates more of the virtual table and continues to page through the "table" until the query is satisfied.

SQL database management systems keep track of views in their data dictionaries. SQLBase tracks views in three tables of its catalog: SYSSYNONYMS, SYSTABLES, and SYSVIEWS. Remember that all SQL DBMSs don't function in exactly the same way. In other words, they may not have the same files that SQLBase does. But they are all similar. The SQLBase SYSVIEWS table contains at least one row for every view in the database. SYSTABLES, the catalog table that tracks database tables, includes views. That allows the DBMS to treat a view, in most cases, as if it were a physical table. And SYSSYNONYMS keeps track of synonyms you assign to views and tables. A synonym is an alias or alternative name for a table or view. Often, it is a short name selected for ease of use in a database application.

Views are, as we said, built upon the data in tables. However, since a view is usually treated as a physical table, many SQL database management systems, including SQLBase, allow you to include views as elements of other views. You or your users don't need to know that a view is a view in order to use it. Simply treat it as any other table in your database.

Data Types

In order to store data in tables, SQL DBMS defines it by data types. The type of data determines how the database management system will handle the data. For example, you would want to treat numbers differently than you would treat text characters. In that case, numbers would imply values while text characters would simply be representations without inherent values. Dates and times, being a sort of hybrid of text and numbers, might be handled differently still.

SQL database management systems are not, as we have seen, all exactly the same. Generally speaking, however, they all have at least three basic data types: character, numeric, and date. Some systems have additional types, such as time. Others have subtypes that further define the broader categories. SQLBase has three main data types: character, number, and data/time. It further subdivides these three types to get more variety and definition.

The character data type in SQLBase is subdivided into CHAR (or VARCHAR) and LONG VARCHAR (or LONG). While this is the SQLBase way of doing things, it is fairly typical, though not always exactly the same, in many other SQL implementations. The CHAR data type must have a character length associated with it. In other, nonSQL databases, it might be called a fixed length character field or type. The data elements of this data type are all characters without numeric value and the elements must not be more than 254 bytes. Any ASCII character may be part of a string of the CHAR type. When defining a data type, you enter the name for the data type with the length in characters in parentheses. For example, you might use CHAR(34) to indicate a data element that could be of the character type up to 34 characters long.

The LONG VARCHAR type is identical to the CHAR type, except that you do not designate the length of the data elements that fit within it. The elements can be any length up to 254 characters. In other types of databases this might be called a variable length character field or type.

SQLBase uses several different number data types: NUMBER, DECIMAL, INTEGER, SMALLINT, FLOAT, REAL, and DOUBLE PRECISION. Up to 15 digits are allowed in the exact data types while -1.0E126 to 1.0E128 are allowed in approximate data types. The exact data types include NUMBER, DECIMAL, INTEGER, and SMALLINT. Approximate data types are FLOAT, REAL, and DOUBLE PRECISION.

The NUMBER data type is a general numeric type that has no defined scale (number of digits to the right of the decimal point) or precision (total number of digits). The DECIMAL (or DEC) type has a defined scale and precision. When you represent this data type, you write DECIMAL (P,S) where S is the scale and P is the precision of the element that will be stored in this type. Thus, if you wanted to represent numbers as currency up to $9,999.00, you would need to type DECIMAL (8,2)—eight digits including the comma and decimal point, and two places to the right of the decimal.

The INTEGER data type has no digits to the right of the decimal. In other words, this type consists of whole numbers only. An INTEGER may be up to ten digits long. SMALLINT is exactly the same as INTEGER except that it may be only five digits long. DOUBLE PRECISION refers to a data type that must contain only double precision, floating point numbers.

The FLOAT data type is a floating point number with the number of digits specified such as: FLOAT (15). If the number of digits is 21 or fewer, the number is presumed to be single precision. From 22 to 53 digits, the number is double precision. If no digits are specified, double precision is assumed. REAL data types contain single precision floating point numbers.

SQLBase uses three subtypes for the date/time data type. DATETIME (or TIMESTAMP) contains both the date and the time. DATE is a date only and TIME is a time only. There are prescribed ways to use these data types as constants in an SQL query. Numbers are always used "as-is," that is, without quotes or other notation of any kind. Strings of characters must be enclosed in quotes. Dates and times may be indicated directly (without quotes).

QUICK SUMMARY

Here are some of the important points in this chapter. The word or phrase in bold lists a relational database feature. That feature's definition and its benefit to you follows.

The data dictionary The data dictionary is a set of "tables of tables." Its system catalog contains the database structure, the structure of each of the tables in the database, all of the indexes and key columns, as well as other pertinent information about the database.

Data types In order to store data in tables, SQL databases define it by data types. The type of data determines how the database management system will handle the data. SQL systems generally speaking, have at least three basic data types: character, numeric, and date.

Primary and foreign keys Primary keys are used to connect two or more tables together. In order for a column to be a primary key, the values in it must be unique to each row. You also can use primary keys to reference columns in the same table. When you have two or more tables, each containing the same column and the same data elements, you can combine or join those tables based upon the data element values in the primary key. The identical columns and data in the subsequent tables are called foreign keys. You can have a foreign key and a primary key within the same table.

SQL databases SQL databases are, actually, collections of tables of data. These tables contain the various data sets that we want to work with for a particular application.

SQL indexes SQL indexes have some major benefits to users. First, they dramatically improve performance. Also, when indexing is done correctly, maintaining integrity and uniqueness of keys, data integrity, and consistency is preserved. Indexing in SQL can be maintained by the database system, so there is no need to designate indexes in advance. Thus there is far less chance of an index not matching actual data in a table than in nonSQL/relational database management systems. However, remember if you leave indexing to the DBMS, you will sacrifice performance.

SQL objects In SQL we refer to the database and its components as objects. SQL objects include the database itself, the tables that make up the database, indexes for the tables, and views that represent data from several tables.

SQL tables SQL uses tables to organize data. They may be actual individual files or they may be included in a larger database file. Each table is unique and has its own name. When you want to retrieve data from a table you refer to it by name. Tables in SQL look like the familiar spreadsheets you have seen in programs like Lotus 1-2-3.

Views A view is not a physical table. It is, instead, a virtual table made up of rows and columns that you select using an SQL query. However, so that you can repeat the view, SQL stores a definition of it in the data dictionary. Thus you can have a view that acts, for all intents and purposes, like a physical table of data. Views differ from physical tables in that they actually don't exist. What does exist is the definition of the view. Therefore, when you query a view (which you can, just as if it were a table) you are actually querying a set of instructions. SQL uses those instructions to build a virtual table.

PRACTICE WHAT YOU'VE LEARNED

1. What is the difference between an SQL database and databases in most other types of database management systems?

2. What are SQL objects?

3. What is query optimizing?

4. Compare SQL tables with a nonSQL database.

5. What is a join?

6. What is referential integrity?

7. What is a referential constraint?

8. What is the main advantage of SQL indexing over indexing in nonSQL/relational databases?

9. What is the purpose of the data dictionary or catalog?

ANSWERS

1. An SQL database is, actually, a collection of tables, views, and indexes. Other database management systems refer to individual data sets as databases.

2. SQL objects include tables, views, and indexes as well as individual data elements and keys.

3. Query optimizing is an operation performed by the database management system that examines your query and prepares it to perform its task. Optimizing includes determining the best combination of indexing and full table search to extract the data requested in the query.

4. NonSQL databases are, often, very similar to SQL tables. In most cases, at least, the intent of the two is the same. They are both discrete collections of data, often arranged in a tabular format.

5. A join is an SQL technique for combining columns of two tables so that a combined query of both tables may be made. The two (or more) tables must have at least one column in common and the rows selected need to meet the criteria of the query. There can be data from both tables in accordance with the columns specified in the query.

6. Referential integrity occurs when the column used as the primary key does not contain data not contained in the column used as a foreign key.

7. If we restrain the foreign key to referencing a specified table, we are enforcing a referential constraint.

8. Index files in databases other than relational ones must list the record numbers in the order inferred from the contents of the key field. When you query such a database, it checks the index file and places the record pointer at the database record containing the value of the key field from the index. This forces you to determine in advance how you plan to set up your indexes and what data fields you will use as key fields. SQL indexing can be done by the database. You determine how you want to access data at the time you form your query. The query optimizer and the DBMS decide how to use the indexes. However, it is always best to create indexes specifically, since the process of forcing the optimizer to create the index results in a loss of performance. Allowing the DBMS to build indexes automatically should be thought of as a "safety net" if your application should require an index you didn't plan for.

9. The data dictionary keeps track of all of the elements in the database, including tables, indexes, keys, views, and users.

The SQL Query

In the past three chapters we have explored the relational database, query techniques, and the structure of an SQL database. We have but one more chapter before we can start building actual SQL queries. This chapter is a sort of bridge between theory and practice. In Chapter 4 you will learn:

▲ How to construct and annotate an SQL query

▲ What an SQL statement is and how to use it

▲ What predicates are and what they do

▲ What an SQL clause is

▲ How to construct subqueries

Now, since we have this bridge to cross, let's put on our walking shoes and get started.

Building the SQL Query

We'll start out our trek by describing the techniques for building and annotating an SQL query. Perhaps you recall, in those dim, nearly forgotten days of elementary school, the techniques of sentence diagramming you learned in English. Earlier in this book we remarked that SQL was an English-like language. As it happens, the similarities are more than superficial. You can diagram an SQL statement in much the same way you used to diagram sentences. The purpose is also the same: to better understand query (or sentence) structure.

While it is true that you don't (and neither will we, except as necessary to explain the syntax of a statement) use SQL syntax diagrams when you are writing "real" SQL statements, you will find that the diagrams help you to understand what is happening within the statement.

There are two opposite schools of thought, both about half right, concerning the difficulty and complexity of SQL as a language. One school declares that SQL is very simple, since it has so few actual commands. The other points to the many ways you can build SQL statements and proclaims that it is an extremely complex language. The fact is that both camps are right. And both are wrong. SQL is far from simple when used to its full power. Its queries can become extraordinarily complex. However, for all of its complexity, it is not a difficult language to learn.

Command Line Structure

Since we are using Gupta's SQLBase as our model, we will also use the Gupta convention for annotating or diagramming SQL syntax. Like everything else about SQL, though, the Gupta way is pretty standard and the deviations you'll find, if any, are trivial. In deference to that convention, then, Figure 4.1 shows a typical syntax diagram, in this case for the CREATE INDEX statement, courtesy of Gupta Technologies.

Syntax diagrams in SQL are similar to sentence diagrams in English grammar. They relate the interaction of command verbs with nouns, modifiers, and phrases. You read these syntax diagrams from upper left to lower right, just as you would an English sentence. Before we discuss what the diagram means, perhaps we should introduce you to the meanings of the individual symbols. Also courtesy of Gupta Technologies, Figure 4.2 provides the explanations.

Now, back to our sample statement and its syntax diagram. As we introduce you to new SQL statements, we will use the syntax diagrams as an aid to illustrate the use of the new command. The name of an SQL command is always a verb. By that we mean that the command name is a verb in the purest sense of an English verb: it is an action word. It tells you (or, in the case of SQL, the program) to do something. Then, as in all good sentences, the verb is followed by modifiers that explain in somewhat more detail just what it is that is expected.

Throughout this book we will signify command or statement names and verbs in the syntax by typing them in UPPERCASE CHARACTERS. Likewise, we will print the statement's keywords in UPPERCASE CHARACTERS. Names of tables, databases, columns, indexes, etc., will be printed in lowercase characters. In our example diagram, then, CREATE is both the command and the verb.

Now, we must know what to CREATE. In this case, we will CREATE and INDEX called index-name. But there are several kinds

▼ *Figure 4.1. Syntax Diagrams in SQL*

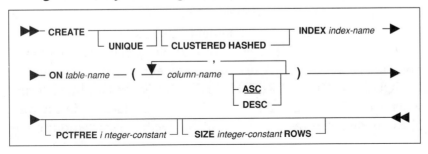

▼ *Figure 4.2. Syntax diagram symbols in Structured Query Language*

▶▶–	The right-pointing double arrow always starts a command.
–▶	The single, right-pointing arrow signals the continuation of the same command on the next line.
◀◀	The left-pointing double arrow always ends a command.
└ UNIQUE ┘	When a command hangs from a line, it is an optional clause or keyword.
ASC / DESC	When optional clauses or keywords are stacked below the main command line, you have the choice of using one or the other. The default choice is underlined.
table-name / view-name	In cases where an alternate is stacked beneath a keyword, you must use one or the other. This signals an alternate choice among mandatory, rather than optional, clauses.
– (▼ column-name ,) –	An arrow that points back to the beginning of an argument means that you can repeat that argument as many times as you like. Delimiters, such as commas, show you how to separate each instance of the argument (for example, column-name, column-name, column-name).

of indexes that we can CREATE. If those types of indexes were either/or choices, they would be shown on top of each other and placed beneath the main line. The default choice (what SQL will do if you don't tell it otherwise), if any, will be the first one under the main line and it will be underscored as in the choice of ASCending or DESCending later in the statement. ASCending is the default.

However, the first choices in the CREATE INDEX statement are not either/or choices. You may have either, both, or neither UNIQUE and CLUSTERED HASHED (we'll explain those terms when we get to the CREATE INDEX command later on in Chapter 5) as optional clauses or keywords. So, we have started our command syntax diagram with a double arrow, indicating the beginning of the statement. Next we state our verb, in this case CREATE. Our next task is to add optional clauses or keywords modifying the object of our statement, INDEX. Finally, on this line we need an index-name to tell SQL what we want the index we are CREATing to be called. Then, since we have more to say, but have run out of room, we terminate the line with a single arrow indicating that at least one more line is to follow.

We open the second line of the statement with another single arrow and add another piece of the main command, in this case ON. Now, if we scan the rest of the diagram, we see that there are no more words on the main line or the lines under it (called continuation lines). Thus we can make an observation that will help us to recall, in the future, the main parts of any SQL statement. If we collect the words from the verb to the end of the whole statement that sit on the main or continuation lines, we have the name of the SQL statement. In this case the statement is CREATE INDEX ON. The verb is CREATE. INDEX and ON are modifiers. We have several different statements that use the same verb: CREATE. But three is only one correct syntax for creating an index: CREATE INDEX ON.

Adding some of the important arguments now becomes pretty simple. For example, we wouldn't be tempted to forget the index's name if we think of the statement as CREATE (what?) INDEX (called what?) index-name. Likewise, if we continue, ON (on what?) table-name. So, by visualizing the syntax diagram and using a bit of common sense, we can pretty well ferret out the major parts of just about any SQL command.

Notice that, up until now, we have used the terms statement and command interchangeably. If we were to be strictly accurate, we would reserve statement for those complex queries that are composed of SQL commands. However, in common parlance, a command and a statement are pretty much the same thing. We'll stick to that convention just to avoid confusion. When we mean one of those complex queries, we'll say what we mean: query.

Returning to our example, we have another argument that is mandatory: column-name. We can tell that an argument is mandatory because it sits on either the main line or a continuation line and it is written in lowercase type. Remember, UPPERCASE for parts of the command or optional clauses, lowercase for arguments. This time the argument is inside parentheses with an arrow pointing backwards with a comma in the middle. That means that you can have more than one column-name separated by commas, but you must have at least one. Following the column-name, or names, you have the option of adding another clause, this time as an either/or choice. If you do nothing, SQL will CREATE an ASCending INDEX.

We're out of space again, so we add another arrow and move on to another continuation line. Now, we have a couple of additional options, but you'll notice that if we select either (or, for that matter, both) of these options, we will have mandatory arguments that go along with the option. We'll discuss the specifics of those arguments and what they mean when we get around to describing the CREATE INDEX ON statement in the next chapter. Once we reach the end of the statement, our syntax diagram terminates with another double arrow pointing, this time, to the left. This double arrow is, in a real statement, the same as a semicolon (;). It reminds us not to forget to terminate our SQL statement.

Statements

The syntax diagram is generic. That means that we don't use it if we have real indexes, column-names, tables, or whatever. We simply use it to illustrate the form of a particular SQL statement. When we start building complex queries, we may also use the diagram to illustrate the complexities of the query, and, one hopes, to simplify understanding. Also, we have rather glossed over the reason for terminating a line and adding a continuation line. We said that we had run out of room. That is not, actually, the full story.

TIP

While there is no hard and fast rule for breaking up an SQL statement, we can think of the line breaks as commas in a real sentence.

For most professional writers, the comma is a place to pause in a sentence. When you pause in a sentence, you usually do so to separate long strings of words or phrases. The pause makes it easier for the reader to "hear" the sentence in his or her mind as he or she reads, and, thus, to clarify the writer's meaning. Line breaks in SQL serve the same purpose. SQL does not need any line breaks at all to function. But people need them to understand the statement more clearly. Thus, line breaks are added to increase readability and understandability of SQL statements and queries.

Now, let's strip away the syntax diagram and, still sticking to our generic example, write the statement that could flow out of the syntax. Notice that we have a few possible choices, since this particular statement allows several options. Here are a couple of possibilities. We'll start with the simplest.

```
CREATE INDEX index-name ON table-name
(column-name);
```

Now, for a bit more complexity:

```
CREATE UNIQUE INDEX index-name
ON table-name (column-name-1, column-name-2);
```

And, finally, all possible options (in a single statement, of course):

```
CREATE UNIQUE CLUSTERED HASHED INDEX
index-name
ON table-name (column-name-1, column-name-2)
PCTFREE integer-constant SIZE integer-
constant ROWS;
```

Any of the above examples would, under the proper circumstances, work just fine. You would correctly be instructing SQL as to the index you want including all of the possible options that the syntax of the command allows. In a real query, of course, you would substitute the actual table name for our table-name, the column names for our column-name-1, column-name-2, etc., and the actual index name for our index-name. The term integer-constant refers to a whole (nondecimal) number such as 1, 2, or 56.

CHECK YOURSELF

1. Build an SQL query for SELECTing all of the CUSTOMERs from the table NEWSALES. (NOTE: All pieces of the statement that you will need are in BOLD UPPERCASE.)

2. Now, narrow your query to include only those CUSTOMERs WHERE the STATE in which they live is MIchigan.

ANSWERS

1. SELECT customer FROM newsales;

2. SELECT customer FROM newsales WHERE state = "MI";

Did you remember the semicolon at the end of the SQL statement and the quotes around MI ("MI")?

Statements, as we have pointed out, are the culmination of the inclusion of several SQL elements into a single SQL "sentence." We have referred to some of these elements in our description of the syntax diagram. Those that we alluded to were verbs, clauses, keywords, and arguments. However, whether it was obvious or not, you have met other elements in the preceding chapters. A couple of those were data types and constants (such as strings or numbers). Just as an English sentence is composed of its own elements (verbs, nouns, adjectives, adverbs, punctuation marks, etc.), so, too, is SQL. Some of its other elements, to which we will now introduce you, are predicates, clauses, and subqueries.

Clauses

We referenced the term clause earlier in the chapter. However, it needs a bit more discussion, so here we go. First, you should understand that a clause is the most indistinct of all SQL elements. It is a sort of catchall term for the general pieces that go into an SQL statement. Like our ever-recurring English sentence, SQL sentences are made of clauses.

Interestingly, you can usually spot an SQL clause because it is likely to begin with a special keyword. Although we will not go into detail on these clauses until Chapter 6, their keywords are:

▲ WHERE
▲ FROM
▲ GROUP BY
▲ HAVING
▲ ORDER BY
▲ UNION

These keywords have special meanings of their own. We usually use them, and the clauses they signal, as part of a SELECT statement, although they do pop up in other SQL statements. Whenever we use them, however, they have pretty much the same meanings. At this point in our tour of SQL we will introduce you to these important keywords and tell you a bit about how you use them. Later, in Chapter 6, we will give more detailed examples of their use with the SELECT verb. You will also see some of them when we discuss other verbs. When we encounter them later on, we will limit our discussions to their use and effects on the particular verb under scrutiny at the time. For now, here are some generic introductions to these important SQL elements.

WHERE

We use the WHERE keyword with the argument search condition to tell SQL how to search a table or view for data. Search conditions are predicates connected by the operator AND, OR, or NOT with AND or OR. Predicates may have elements compared to each other such as one value that equals another (A = B), or, perhaps, one that does not equal another (A < > B).

Often, the WHERE keyword signals a search condition consisting of a single predicate. So, we could have

A = B OR A = C

as a complex search condition consisting of two predicates in the clause, or we could have

A = B

as a simple search condition. In either case, A, B, or C could be constants (actual numeric or string values) or they could be data in an SQL table (column-name-1 = column-name-2). They could be combinations of the two as well (column-name = 5). Whatever the search condition, the WHERE keyword signals that a clause intended to locate some data is on the way.

FROM

The FROM keyword starts a clause that will tell you in which table or view data is being sought resides. You can use a kind of shorthand for the table name in a FROM clause called a correlation name. The correlation name is, simply, the first character (or, if necessary, some other simple combination of characters) of the table name. Of course the correlation names in a single FROM clause must be unique.

This is a good time to digress and discuss, briefly, a piece of common SQL notation. You may have noticed that we have referred to column-name throughout this chapter. We have sort of led you to believe that column names are unique and within a single table for the purposes of forming an SQL query. However that is not always (in fact, it usually isn't) the case. We often use columns from several tables. That, of course, is one of SQL's strongest points: its ability to work with multiple tables. So we need a method of notation that allows us to specify both the table and the column names.

That method is, fortunately, simplicity itself. We simply write the table name in front of the column name and separate the two with a period (.) thusly:

table-name.column-name

That means that we can substitute the correlation name in a query if we have previously defined it in the query. The place to do the defining is in the FROM clause, and we can then use it in the WHERE clause, like this: FROM table-name-1 correlation-name-1, table-name-2 correlation-name-2 WHERE correlation-name-1.column-name = correlation-name-2.column-name;

In this example, the column names in the two tables are the same. Note where we used commas and where we did not.

TIP

The placement of punctuation in SQL statements is very important. Your SQL statements will not work if you are sloppy with your punctuation, especially the semicolon at the end of the statement.

GROUP BY

You may recall that, much earlier, we discussed result sets. We told you that they are the virtual tables created when you perform a query. We may want to keep all rows of our result set grouped together by some criteria. For example, if our query was intended to gather the names of all customers by the state in which they live, we would be GROUPing BY state. If the customers each represented a row in our table and the states were columns, we could group the rows (customers) by a particular column (state) using a GROUP BY clause.

HAVING

You use clauses beginning with the HAVING keyword with clauses beginning with the GROUP BY keyword. HAVING lets you add a search condition to the GROUP BY clause. So, in our example above (GROUP customers BY state) we could add an additional qualifier, perhaps that the customer did more than one million dollars of business with our company. We would, of course, need a column called sales, or something like that, to hold the sales figure. We could then GROUP customers HAVING sales greater than 1,000,000 BY state.

ORDER BY

ORDER BY allows you to sort the rows in your result set by the values appearing in a specified column. For example, we could ORDER the list of customers from our previous examples, BY sales. Thus, we would end up with a list of customers GROUPed BY state, such that the customers appearing in our result set all had sales of more than one million dollars and the listing would be in order from the lowest to the highest sales figure (unless we specified DESCending).

UNION

UNION is a tough clause to understand at this point in our discussions. For that reason, we're going once over lightly in our explanation with the promise that, later on in Chapter 6, the light will fully dawn. Let's start with the idea that there is an SQL command (probably the most important of all SQL commands, actually) called SELECT. The purpose of SELECT is to extract data from one or more tables. How you construct the SELECT command is, really, what SQL is all about. As you will soon see, the complexity that SQL mavens refer to is pretty much all tied up in the SELECT verb. It is the most powerful and, thus, the most useful command in the entire SQL syntax.

When you perform a SELECT, you create a result set. The clauses we have been discussing add power and selectivity to the SELECT verb. Once you have completed your SELECT statement, including all of the clauses, predicates, keywords, and other miscellany, you will have built a virtual result set.

Now, if you do the same thing all over (a different query this time) you can merge the results of those two SELECTs into a single result set with duplicate rows removed. The mechanism used to merge these two SELECTs is the UNION clause. Of course, you are performing the two SELECTs within a single query. The two parts of the complete query are connected by the UNION keyword and you can add an ORDER BY clause to the UNION clause to produce a final result set order. We'll get into UNION a bit more deeply in Chapter 7 when we discuss complex queries.

These are the keywords that point to a special clause within an SQL query. The purpose of these clauses is to allow you to narrow the scope of your query until you have zeroed in on exactly the data you need. As you may begin to see, it is far easier to extract data from one or more tables by building an SQL sentence than by using a series of complicated procedural programming steps.

CHECK YOURSELF

1. What is an SQL clause?

2. What are the keywords that point to clauses in SQL?

3. Why do we need clauses?

ANSWERS

1. A clause is the most indistinct of all SQL elements. It is a sort of catchall term for the general pieces that go into an SQL statement. Like our ever-recurring English sentence, SQL sentences are made of clauses.

2. WHERE, FROM, GROUP BY, HAVING, ORDER BY, and UNION are SQL keywords that point to clauses.

3. The purpose of clauses is to allow you to narrow the scope of your query until you have zeroed in on exactly the data you need.

Predicates

Predicates, as we said earlier, are direct comparisons between two elements, expressions, or conditions. There are six basic kinds of predicates. As in our discussion of clauses we will limit our descriptions to the basic, leaving the detailed for later on as the need presents itself. The six kinds of predicates are:

▲ Relational
▲ BETWEEN
▲ NULL
▲ EXISTS
▲ LIKE
▲ IN

You will notice, no doubt, that one of these is a type while the others look a bit like keywords. That is exactly the case. Relational predicates are the same ones you have known since high school algebra as operators. The rest are, indeed, SQL keywords. As such you will find them embedded within SQL statements and clauses. Let's start with the Relational predicate.

Relational

There are two types of Relational predicates. One, the Quantified Relational predicate, involves a device called a subquery. Subqueries are important enough to deserve their own explanation. We will have to wait for that description until a bit later in this chapter. However, the other kind of Relational predicate, the Comparison Relational predicate, is well within the scope of our current discussion.

Comparison Relational predicates are nothing more than the comparison of two values using the traditional relational operators:

▲   = Equal to
▲   != or <> Not equal to
▲   > Greater than
▲   !> Not greater than
▲   < Less than
▲   !< Not less than
▲   >= Greater than or equal to
▲   <= Less than or equal to

For example, we could create a predicate where the value of a column must not equal 5. It would look something like this:

column-name <> (or, if you prefer, !=) 5

Although this may seem a bit simplistic, it is really all there is to it. Remember, when using these operators with strings, you must place the literal strings within either single or double quotes. It doesn't matter which type of quotes you use, but both the opening and closing quotes must be of the same type, such as:

column-name = 'Chattanooga, TN'

BETWEEN

The BETWEEN predicate places a value within (or outside of, if you add NOT) a range of values. The predicate looks like this:

value-sought BETWEEN value-1 AND value-2

Or it can look like this:

value-sought NOT BETWEEN value-1 AND value-2

NULL

NULL is an interesting predicate. You use NULL to test for a null value. That is not quite as obvious an explanation as it seems. Null does not equal zero. Zero is, actually, a value—a number with a value of zero. Depending upon where a zero sits within a number, it can have a very important value.

Null, on the other hand, is the absence of a value. Null means that, within a field, column, row, or whatever, there is nothing—not zero—nothing. The NULL predicate tests to see if there is nothing in the element it is testing. If it finds zero, it sees that there is something there (a value of zero) and returns a false. So you can equate a null value to nothing, while a value of zero is, actually, something. Of course, if it saw any other value it would also return a false indication. You can use NOT with NULL to reverse the process.

TIP

If you mean for a value to be zero, you must so state. Simply leaving out the value does not give you a value of zero.

EXISTS

EXISTS tests for existence of a value. Usually EXISTS is used with a WHERE clause as part of a subquery, so we'll have to wait a bit to learn how it can be used. The reason for the delay in explanation is that EXISTS gets its knowledge of whether or not a value exists by performing a type of subquery called a subselect. Subselects are nothing more than SELECTs that occur within a complex query.

LIKE

The LIKE predicate allows you to search for strings that match a predetermined pattern. You can use the % sign wildcard or the underscore (_) to match unknown characters within a pattern. The % matches multiple characters (like the DOS *) and the underscore matches a single character. Thus we could search for the author's name (Stephenson) using either %steph% or steph_ _ _ _ _. You match the contents of a column-name to the target string. NOT is permitted. If our example above was a search for the name within a column called Name, the usage could be:

name LIKE %steph%

IN

You can use the IN predicate when you have built a result set using a subselect clause and you want to compare a value to those in the result table. The IN predicate can get a bit complex, since it can involve subqueries, constants, user lists, expressions, or a new kind of variable called a bind variable.

Bind variables are another shorthand method of SQL notation. They consist of a colon (:) followed by a number or other short notation. The first bind variable in an expression might be :1, the next :2, and so on. The bind variable refers to an instance of data in an SQL statement. You enter the data that SQL will use to replace the bind variables on separate lines after the SQL command. The start of the data is represented by a backslash on a line by itself, the end of the replacement data by a slash on a line by itself after the data.

Bind variables don't need quotes around them even if they are strings. You separate items on a line of data by commas. Basically, the bind variable allows you to build an SQL statement with bind variables instead of actual data, create a list of the data you would use if you didn't have bind variables, and repeat the SQL command automatically for every line of data in your list. By using bind variables you don't have to rewrite the SQL statement for every set of constants in your list. If this seems confusing, don't be concerned at this point. We'll see in more detail how bind variables work in real examples later in Chapter 7. What is important to understand at this point is that a bind variable is a shorthand method that allows you to process an SQL statement repetitively using different data without rewriting the statement over and over.

But, back to the IN predicate. IN simply lets you designate a set of data (or, if you prefer, a list of data items such as variables, constants, or whatever) and check to see if a value you select is included within that list. You can use NOT with IN to test for data items outside the list.

CHECK YOURSELF

1. What is an SQL predicate?

2. Name the SQL keywords that point to a predicate.

3. What is the difference between NULL and ZERO?

ANSWERS

1. Predicates are direct comparisons between two elements, expressions, or conditions.

2. BETWEEN, NULL, EXISTS, LIKE, and IN are SQL keywords that indicate a predicate. Relational is a type of predicate that allows a boolean comparison between two values.

3. NULL is the absence of a value in a column. ZERO is a value of, for lack of a better term, nothing. ZERO could be a numeric value of 0 or it could be a space (" ") in a string.

Subqueries

Subqueries are both simple and complex. They are simple to explain and simple in the theory of what they do. They can, as you will see in Chapter 7, become quite complex. The simple description of an SQL subquery is that it is an additional SELECT statement nested beneath another SELECT statement. In order to distinguish the subquery from the rest of the statement, the first SELECT statement that appears in the query is called the outer query or outer SELECT. Then all of the additional SELECTs that appear in the query (on lines under the outer SELECT) are the subSELECTs or subqueries.

The subqueries execute before the outer query, starting at the bottom of the nest (the last subSELECT in the statement). When a subSELECT returns a single value for use with the outer SELECT the process is a simple subquery. However, if the outer query returns a result set containing more than a single data item, the subquery must execute once for every row in the result set. It is then called a correlated subquery.

The point of subqueries is that, by starting with a fairly broad range of possibilities for a result set, you can narrow the range considerably, usually within a single SQL statement by using sub-queries and, as you will see later, joins. Thus, data residing within multiple tables becomes as one single block of information from which you can pick and choose at will. Based upon that statement, by the way, you might wonder why not simply use a single large table that contains every bit of useful or possibly useful data. The answer to that is twofold. First, database performance would suffer if it needed to search and index huge data tables. Second, you need to combine similar information into tables so that you can identify data that has some inherent logical relationship. Although you will use multiple tables often, much of the data you will seek will be correlated and should, for ease of handling and efficiency of execution, reside together in single, manageable tables.

QUICK SUMMARY

Here are some of the important points in this chapter. The word or phrase in bold lists a relational database feature. That feature's definition and its benefit to you follows.

Syntax diagrams Use syntax diagrams as an aid to illustrate the use of an SQL command.

SQL commands The name of an SQL command is always a verb. That means that the command name is an action word. It tells the program to do something. Then the verb is followed by modifiers that explain in somewhat more detail just what it is that is expected.

Line breaks in SQL People need line breaks to understand the query more clearly. We add line breaks to increase readability and understandability of SQL statements and queries.

SQL clauses A clause is a catchall term for the general pieces that go into an SQL statement. An SQL clause is likely to begin with a special keyword.

Clause keywords WHERE, FROM, GROUP BY, HAVING, ORDER BY, and UNION.

SQL predicates Predicates are direct comparisons between two elements, expressions, or conditions. The six predicates are: Relational, BETWEEN, NULL, EXISTS, LIKE, and IN.

Relational predicates There are two types of Relational predicates. The Quantified Relational predicate involves a subquery. Comparison Relational predicates are the comparison of two values using the traditional relational operators.

NULL Null does not equal zero. Zero is a value—a number with a value of zero. Null is the absence of a value. Null means that, within a field, column, row, or whatever, there is nothing. The NULL predicate tests to see if there is nothing in the element it is testing.

Subqueries The simple description of an SQL subquery is that it is an additional SELECT statement nested beneath another SELECT statement. Subqueries execute before the outer query, starting at the bottom of the nest (the last subSELECT in the statement).

Correlated subqueries When a subSELECT returns a single value for use with the outer SELECT the process is a simple subquery. However, if the outer query returns a result set containing more than a single data item, the subquery must execute once for every row in the result set. It is then called a correlated subquery.

PRACTICE WHAT YOU'VE LEARNED

QUERY REQUIREMENT	CORRECT SQL SYNTAX
1. Build a simple SQL statement that SELECTs USERs FROM a table called customers.	SELECT USER FROM CUSTOMERS;
2. Narrow the SELECTion to only those USERs who use the PRODUCT SQLBASE.	SELECT USER FROM CUSTOMERS WHERE PRODUCT = "SQLBASE";

3. Now, further narrow the query to those USERs in OHio OR INdiana.

SELECT USER
WHERE PRODUCT=
"SQLBASE" and
WHERE STATE = "OH" or
WHERE STATE = "IN";

4. Add USERs of the PRODUCT DBASE IV.

SELECT USER
WHERE PRODUCT =
 "SQLBASE" or
WHERE PRODUCT =
 "DBASE IV" and
WHERE STATE = "OH" or
WHERE STATE = "IN";

5. GROUP the users BY PRODUCT.

SELECT USER
WHERE PRODUCT =
 "SQLBASE" or
WHERE PRODUCT =
 "DBASE IV" and
WHERE STATE = "OH" or
WHERE STATE = "IN"
GROUP BY PRODUCT;

6. ORDER the users BY STATE.

SELECT USER
WHERE PRODUCT =
"SQLBASE" or WHERE
PRODUCT = "DBASE IV"
and
WHERE STATE = "OH" or
WHERE STATE = "IN"
GROUP BY PRODUCT
ORDER BY PRODUCT;

Defining a Database

The first step in the process of building an SQL application is planning and defining the database. In this chapter you will learn the basics of database planning and design. We will also introduce you to the first of the SQL statements you will need: CREATE. This chapter will show you:

- ▲ **How to plan your database**
- ▲ **Some basics about SQLBase as our SQL model**
- ▲ **How to use CREATE to build databases, tables, indexes, synonyms, and views**
- ▲ **How to use DROP database, table, index, synonym, and view**
- ▲ **How to use ALTER TABLE to change the tables in your database**

Planning Your Database

As we told you earlier, the concept of a database in SQL is a bit different from the concept of a database in other, nonrelational or nonSQL systems. In a nonSQL system, database actually refers to that entity that SQL calls a table. In systems like dBASE, you form relations between databases. However, these relations are not the same as those you will form using SQL. In some regards, the results are similar, but the mechanism is different.

In SQL systems, we form relations between tables. The tables for a particular application are defined as part of a database. A database in SQL is a coherent collection of all of the data that your application uses. Whereas you might use different databases in dBASE to collect data for different aspects of your application, in SQL you'll use tables. Here's an example of what we mean.

Suppose that you are creating an accounting application. You'll want to collect name, address, and phone number data on your customers and suppliers. You'll want to keep track of what your customers owe you and what you owe your suppliers. You may want to track your inventory. Perhaps you want to have a module that creates invoices and another that creates purchase orders. It would not be practical to collect all of these data in a single database or table. So you build a separate database (in a dBASE system) or table (in an SQL system) for each aspect of your application.

You would make one table for customers with names, addresses, and phone numbers (you may want to collect more information) and another for suppliers with similar information. You'll make another table for invoices and another for purchases. Those might be accounts receivable and payable. Notice that we have used the term "table" here. That's because we are talking about an SQL application. All of those tables are part of your accounting application's database. If we were talking about a dBASE application we would substitute the term "database" for "table."

The point is that, before you can begin seriously building your application, you need to do a bit of planning. That planning starts with defining the tables you will include in your application's database. As you define the tables, you will also define their contents. Once you have decided what tables you will need and what you will put in them, you can use the CREATE TABLE command to build the tables you need. You can, of course, always use the ALTER TABLE command to change the contents of a table after you have built it if you forgot something. However, it's a good idea to avoid that by carefully thinking out the tables your application needs before you start.

Planning Your Database

SQLBase as a Model

We chose SQLBase as a model for several reasons. First, it is one of the most popular SQL systems for personal computers. Second, it follows industry standards very closely. Third, it offers direct connections into other industry standard SQL systems such as DB2. However, there are some minor, but important, differences between SQLBase and other systems. We alluded to these differences in an earlier chapter when we told you that there were many implementations of SQL.

For example, there are several "housekeeping" commands that SQLBase calls database administration. These commands, like all SQLBase commands, are executed interactively using the SQLTalk utility. If you embed SQLBase in an application, you won't use SQLTalk. Some SQL systems use a similar method, called an SQL editor, for communicating interactively with the database.

Most of SQLTalk's commands may be thought of correctly as SQL commands or statements, while some are unique to SQLTalk. For example, the CREATE DATABASE statement is a typical SQL command while INSTALL DATABASE is not. The functionality provided by SQLTalk's INSTALL DATABASE command is, often, provided by other system's START DATABASE statement (see Figure 5.1).

In order to keep things reasonably consistent for you, we suggest that you read carefully the functionality of a command and match it to similar functionality in your database management system if you are not using SQLBase. In most cases the statement will be the same or very close. Since this is not a book that intends to teach you SQLBase, we will not dwell upon those commands

---

▼ *Figure 5.1. Install (Create) a database in SQLBase's Windows environment, SQLTalk/Windows*

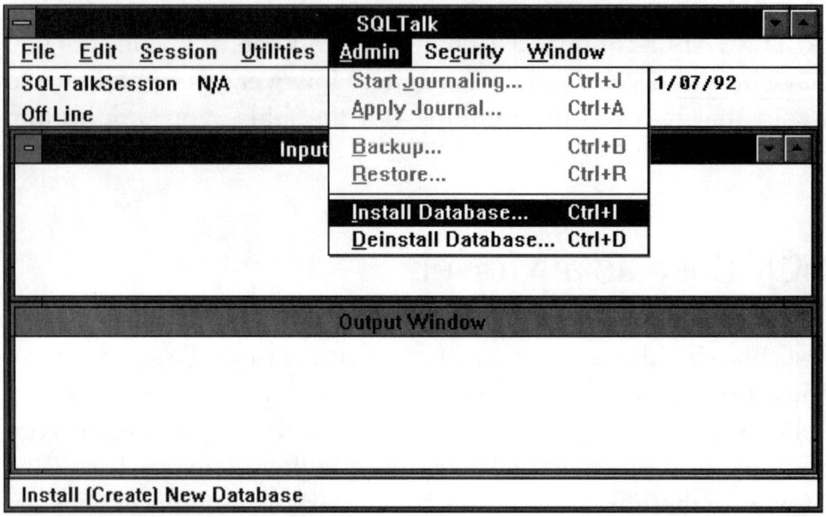

that are unique to SQLTalk or are not part of the standard SQL syntax. For the most part, we will concentrate on standard SQL or the SQLBase version thereof.

Another area we won't involve ourselves in is SQL functions. Functions are like miniprograms that return a value. For example, we might have a function that, when applied to a string of characters, returns the same string in all uppercase characters. In effect, this function, @UPPER in SQLBase, is a miniprogram that looks at each character in the string and, if it is lowercase, changes it to uppercase and replaces the old lowercase character with the new uppercase one.

The reason we will ignore functions is that they differ widely in both syntax and type from SQL database management system to system. Suffice it to say that most SQL implementations have a set of functions. All functions work pretty much the same way, that is, they perform some action or calculation on a piece of data and return a value for the application to use. What differs from implementation to implementation is the set of functions that the implementation supports and the syntax of the functions.

Remember, as we present our examples, what you see on your computer screen may differ slightly from what we tell you to expect. However, regardless of the implementation you are using, you'll find that your results are usually quite close to ours. That's one of the beauties of SQL.

Now that we have discussed, however briefly, the concept of preplanning your database tables and a few things to watch for as we use SQLBase as our model, let's move on to our first SQL command. Remember, we are using the syntax of SQLTalk as the interactive component of SQLBase. You may need to write these commands in your SQL editor, if your system has one. And you will probably want to check your system's syntax if you're not using SQLBase, just to be sure that you've got it exactly right. Now, the big moment is here. Let's move from theory to practice.

Planning Your Database

CREATE

CREATE is an SQL command that, like many other commands, is the basis for a family of SQL statements. As you will notice throughout this book, there are many such "core" statements that, when used with keywords, clauses, or predicates, make up a full family of statements. The core word (CREATE, in this case) is the verb. When used with any of several modifiers of any of several kinds, the verb takes on expanded meaning.

For example, as you will see very shortly, you can CREATE any of several SQL elements depending upon how you build your statement. You can CREATE a database (in SQLBase the command is "INSTALL," see Figure 5.2.). Or, if you prefer, you can CREATE a table, index, synonym, or view. In each case the basic statement consists of the verb (CREATE) and some object. Depending upon what it is you want to CREATE, there may also be predicates or other clauses.

You use CREATE (object) when you want to build (define) the object from scratch. You don't use it to modify an existing object. Thus, if you CREATE a DATABASE, the assumption is that, at the moment, the DATABASE does not exist. You are building a new one. Likewise, CREATE doesn't place the object in use. Depending upon the object, you will use another method to make use of your object. All CREATE does is, well, create the object so you can use it later in your application.

CREATE DATABASE

SYNTAX: CREATE DATABASE database name;

EXAMPLE: CREATE DATABASE accounts;

CREATE DATABASE is a very simple command that has no additional keywords, predicates, or clauses. A database is, in most systems, physically a directory that contains the individual files that are the tables, data dictionary, and other required elements (depending upon the DBMS you are using). Thus, in most systems, the length of the database name is consistent with the directory naming conventions for the operating system under which the DBMS is to be used. In the case of SQLBase, the database name is eight or fewer characters. This is consistent with MS- or PC-DOS.

Once you have CREATEd the DATABASE, you will need to open it in order to use it. This is one of those actions that differs widely from system to system. For example, in some DBMSs you START the database. In others you OPEN it. In SQLBase (SQLTalk, actually) you CONNECT to it (see Figure 5.3). However you get access to the database, though, you must create it first. You will not be able to CREATE any tables, views, indexes, or synonyms without a database open to hold them first. And, whether you have a

▼ *Figure 5.2. Using the SQLTalk/Windows interface for creating the Accounts database*

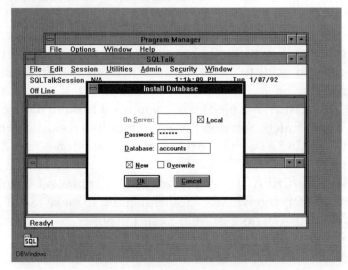

▼ *Figure 5.3. Opening a database by using the SQLTalk CONNECT command*

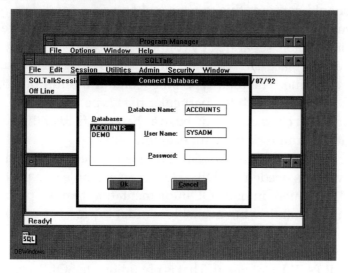

database created or not, unless you open it, you still won't be able to use it or any of its tables or other elements.

One final word on CREATing DATABASEs. It is a good idea to name your database so that the name is descriptive of the database management application. For example, if your application is to be the accounting system to which we referred earlier, you might name the database Accounts or something similar. That way, if you have several DBMS applications on your database server or PC, you'll have no trouble telling which is which. In systems that equate a database to a directory, you'll also add the advantage of collecting all of your DBMS files for a particular application into a single directory with an easily identifiable name.

CREATE TABLE

SYNTAX: CREATE TABLE table name (column name data type,)

IN DATABASE database name;

EXAMPLE: CREATE TABLE payables (sup_name CHAR (30). inv_no INTEGER NOT NULL. inv_amt DECIMAL (8,2),inv_date DATE);

There are a couple of aspects to the CREATE TABLE command that demand extra explanation. First, the column name data type (you should consider this to read "column name and data type") is, actually, a list of the column names and their respective data types in the table separated by commas. For ease of reading, it is a good idea to place each column name and its associated data type on its own line. The data type must contain the full descriptive syntax associated with the particular data type. That could mean the number of characters allowed in a character field or the number of digits in a numeric field, for example.

Second, the IN DATABASE clause is not needed in SQLBase. However, it is needed for DB2. Here is an example of a portion of an SQL statement in one SQL implementation that is optional for that implementation, but available in order to preserve compatibility with another implementation.

Notice that we used the NOT NULL modifier in our example CREATE TABLE statement. That is not unique to SQLBase, but not all SQL implementations use it. NOT NULL in the CREATE TABLE statement means that, whenever you add a row to your table (as you enter data into the table), you must have an entry for that column. In our example that means that you must always include an invoice number (the inv_no column) when you enter new data into the table. This has the effect of making the inv_no field in the data input form (what the user sees in our accounting application) mandatory.

Now that we have brought up the subject of data input forms, let's digress momentarily and discuss them a bit. When you build a business application for other people to use, you use some method of making it "friendly." Usually that means embedding your SQL database in an application written in some other language. We will discuss such applications a bit later on in this book. However, many SQL implementations have tool kits that allow you to build applications without programming in a high level language such as C or Pascal. SQLBase is such an implementation.

Using SQLWindows, you can build very respectable user-friendly applications around your SQL database. One element of such applications is the data input form. The data input form is a method that we use to allow users to enter new data into our SQL table. As its name implies, it looks like a familiar paper business form that we might fill out if we were collecting the data manually.

We create blank spaces on the form called fields. Each of those fields corresponds to a column in our table. We can place an identifying or descriptive name in front of each field to help our user figure out what information to enter into it. That field name is usually far easier to understand than the somewhat cryptic column names we use in our tables. For example, even though the column name we are using in our example is inv_no, the field name on the data input form might be Invoice Number. That would be a lot easier for users to figure out than inv_no.

Also remember that a null in a column is not a value. Rather, it is the absence of a value. A null is not a zero. So, if you want a default value in your NOT NULL column, but you don't want to make the entry of data into the column mandatory, some implementations such as SQLBase allow you to have a NOT NULL WITH DEFAULT column. That means that there will be a default value placed into the column when you create each new row. Remember that you create a new row each time you enter new data (using the INSERT command) into the table.

The value of the default depends upon the implementation. In SQLBase the default for a numeric column is zero (not null). For a date column it is the current system date or time—the date or time when you create the row. And for a character column, it is a null. This capability is compatible with DB2.

Planning Your Database

CHECK YOURSELF

What You Should Do	How the Computer Responds
Start SQLBase and SQLTalk and open the DEMO database.	You'll see the SQL> prompt
Type: CREATE TABLE test (name CHAR (30), age INTEGER, dob DATE);	TABLE CREATED

Type: 0 ROWS SELECTED
SELECT * FROM test;

Notice that you created the new table (test) with three columns (name, age, and dob—date of birth). Once you created the table you tried to list all of the data in the table using the SELECT command. Since you hadn't entered any data, SQLBase did not select any rows. From now on, we'll provide a bit less explanation in our exercises and self-checks.

CREATE INDEX

SYNTAX: CREATE UNIQUE INDEX index-name
ON table-name (column-name ASC/DESC,);

EXAMPLE: CREATE UNIQUE INDEX invoices
ON payables (inv_date DESC, inv_no);

It's time to discuss indexes a bit more. If you recall, we said that an index is a special table that tells our DBMS the order we want to use to search a data table. In other words, if we want to see all of our customers in alphabetical order, rather than sorting the table and creating a whole new table in that order, we simply build an index. The index tells the DBMS that we want to look at the customer column and order all of the rows by the contents of that column. The DBMS then creates a special index file and uses it whenever we want to go after customer names to speed the search.

We also said that many SQL DBMS can create an index on the fly so that we never need be without an index. But we emphasized that it is far more efficient to build the indexes in advance so that the DBMS doesn't need to do it for us. It is the CREATE INDEX statement that we use to specify our indexes.

There are several parts to the CREATE INDEX statement. We have included only those that are fairly consistent from SQL implementation to implementation. There are, in other implementations, additional keywords and clauses that are not consistent across all implementations of SQL.

The first optional keyword is UNIQUE. You do not need UNIQUE in the statement if you do not wish to enforce unique key values within a table. That means that, if you use UNIQUE, each value that you enter into the column on which you are building the index must be unique. If this index is to be a primary key, you will probably use UNIQUE. Otherwise, unless you have a specific reason, you probably won't. In our example we use UNIQUE because we don't want to allow more than one invoice to have the same invoice number.

Planning Your Database

TIP

Use UNIQUE to insure that users don't enter the same value into an index column twice.

The column-name entry can, actually, be several columns separated by commas, as in our example. In our example we wanted to order our payables table first by the invoice date (inv_date) and, within any given date, by the invoice number (inv_no). So we set the first column-name as inv_date and the second as inv_no.

Indexes can be either in ASCending or DESCending order. The default is ASCending. In our example, however, we wanted to show the most recent date first and work our way back to the oldest invoices. So we specified DESCending. If we had wanted ASCending ordering, we could have left out the keyword altogether. That's what we did with the invoice numbers. That means that, on any given date, the first invoice for that date will appear first and the last will appear last.

CREATE SYNONYM

SYNTAX: CREATE SYNONYM synonym-name FOR table-/view-name;

EXAMPLE: CREATE SYNONYM ap FOR payables;

A synonym is, really, no more than a shorthand method of referring to a table or view (see Figure 5.4).

Depending upon the implementation of SQL, it may also be a method of permitting users to access a table in certain circumstances that they otherwise could not access due to user access rights. Here's what that means.

▼ *Figure 5.4. Creating a synonym*

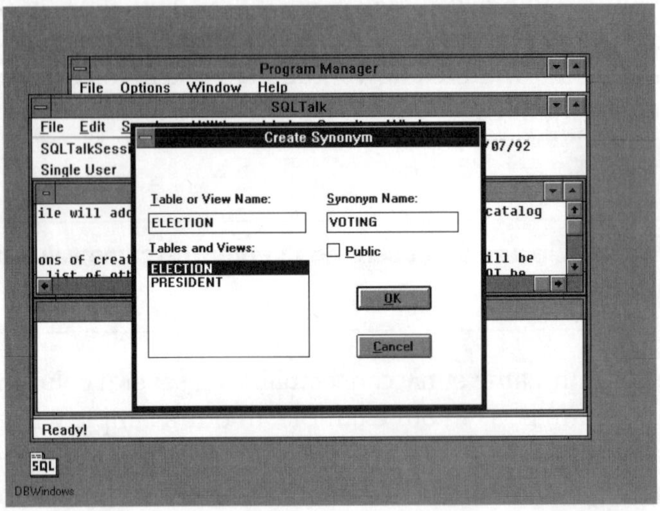

Some implementations of SQL, including SQLBase, allow you to attach an authorization ID to the tables you create. Essentially that means that you, as the owner (creator) of a table, are deciding who can and cannot have access to the table. When you CREATE the table, you CREATE it with the authorization ID as part of the table name. Only users with the rights to that authorization ID can access the table.

Of course there may be times when you want other users to access the table for a particular well-defined and well-controlled task. So you create a synonym for that table and allow those otherwise unauthorized users access to the synonym. When you want them to use the restricted table, you specify the synonym instead of the actual table name. Thus, you can, under careful control, allow your users to have it both ways: allowed access when you want and disallowed when you don't. And you can provide that capability without the overhead of changing user access rights.

That's one use for synonyms. Another is, simply, to provide a shorthand for use within the application without sacrificing the clarity of more detailed table or view names. A third reason for synonyms is to allow you to define a table or view based upon how you are using it in the application. That way, as you scan through the listings of your commands (when you embed SQL in an application) you can quickly determine how you were using a table or view by the synonym you gave it.

CHECK YOURSELF

What You Should Do	**How the Computer Responds**
Start SQLBase and SQLTalk	SQL>
Type: INSERT INTO test (name, age, dob) VALUES ('peter', 47, 05-may-1944);	1 ROW INSERTED
SELECT * FROM test;	NAME AGE DOB ================== peter 47 05-MAY-1944 1 ROW SELECTED
CREATE SYNONYM names FOR test;	SYNONYM CREATED
SELECT * FROM names;	NAME AGE DOB ================== peter 47 05-MAY-1944 1 ROW SELECTED

CREATE VIEW

   SYNTAX: CREATE VIEW view-name (column-name,)
AS select;

   EXAMPLE: CREATE VIEW invoices
AS SELECT inv_date, inv_no, sup_name
FROM payables
WHERE inv_amt > 0;

   We haven't quite got enough information yet to get particularly exotic with the AS select portion of this statement. However, here, in simple terms for the moment, is what it means. We are going to create a virtual table from a real table with only some of the data contained in the real table. By a virtual table we mean that we won't create a real, physical table. Instead, we will set out the instructions to create such a physical table if we were going to do so. This is much like our indexing. We don't create a real table containing all of our data rearranged by the rules of our index. Instead, we create a set of rules as if we were going to do that. We call that an index.

We do the same thing with a view. We set out the rules for our new table. The rules define the view. When we need the data the view has to offer, instead of creating a whole new table, we use our rules (the view definition) to create a virtual table with all that information. This technique can be remarkably useful when we frequently want to look at data arranged a particular way. We can define the data we want to see in our view and, no matter what data has been added since we defined the view, we'll get only the data that meets our criteria (as defined in the CREATE VIEW statement).

In our example, we decided that we wanted to see (no matter when we asked) only those invoices that were still open (with inv_amt greater than zero). Basically we want to see which suppliers we still owe money to. Also, we don't need to see all of the information in the table, just the invoice number, date, and supplier. So we create a new view of the payables table, which we name Invoices. In our view we show only the inv_date, inv_no, and sup_name columns. Finally we include a WHERE clause that limits the rows SELECTed to those where the inv_amt is greater than zero. That, of course, assumes that we zero out that column when we pay the supplier. That would leave only those rows where we still owed some money in our view.

There is another use for a view that is even more important. As you will learn later, we can use the SELECT clause to combine SELECTed columns of more than one table to get a composite table containing some columns from each of those tables. If we are performing that join only occasionally, we can write out the complete statement each time we need it. However, if we are performing the join frequently, it becomes quite tedious to continually rewrite the command. So we do it once and use it to define a view. From then on, we can use the view as if it were a physical table.

We'll discuss joins in detail in Chapter 7. However, for now, you should realize that the SELECT statement can be used as a clause in certain other SQL statements. When we use SELECT in that manner it is called a subselect clause. In most cases the syntax of the subselect is the same as the syntax for SELECT. You will learn the syntax and uses for SELECT in the next chapter.

DELETE DATABASE

SYNTAX: DELETE DATABASE database-name;

EXAMPLE: DELETE DATABASE accounts;

This, like the CREATE DATABASE statement, is a simple one. It is, in fact, its opposite. When you want to wipe out a database, you use this command. Unlike DEINSTALL DATABASE, which only removes the database name from your database server, DE-LETE DATABASE actually wipes out all data, tables, views, and data dictionary entries. In short, when you DELETE a DATABASE, it's gone forever. DELETE DATABASE is, as is CREATE DATABASE, a part of SQLTalk. It is not, in SQLBASE, anyway, considered part of the SQL command set. In some other implementations, however, it is.

DROP TABLE, INDEX, SYNONYM, AND VIEW

SYNTAX: DROP TABLE/VIEW/INDEX/SYNONYM name;

EXAMPLE: DROP TABLE payables;

Here's another command, or, rather, family of commands that are pretty straightforward and simple. When you DROP a table, synonym, view, or index all you are doing is removing that element from the database and, thus, the data dictionary (see Figure 5.5). However, depending upon the element you are DROPping, you may also affect other elements.

For example, if you DROP a TABLE, you will also delete all views, indexes, and synonyms that reference the table. If you DROP a VIEW, you'll also delete any other views that use the view you DROPped. Likewise, if you DROP a SYNONYM, you will also

▼ *Figure 5.5. Example database showing the DROP command*

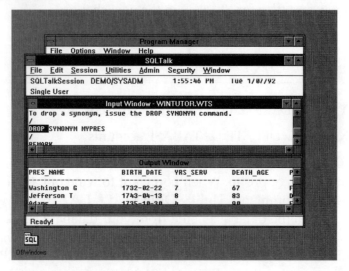

delete views based upon the synonym. You cannot, however, DROP any of the data dictionary tables or any views or synonyms that use them. Also, in most SQL implementations, you must either be the database administrator or you must specifically own the elements you are DROPping.

ALTER TABLE

SYNTAX: ALTER TABLE table-name
DROP column-name, column-name
ADD column-name data type NOT NULL/NOT NULL WITH DEFAULT,
RENAME column-name new name,/TABLE new name
MODIFY column-name data type (length) NULL/NOT NULL/NOT NULL WITH DEFAULT,;

EXAMPLE: ALTER TABLE payables
DROP sup_name
ADD sup_lname CHAR (20), sup_fname CHAR (20);

ALTER TABLE allows you to add, delete or modify the columns in a table (Figure 5.6). You can also rename columns or the table

▼ *Figure 5.6. ALTER TABLE command in SQLTalk Windows*

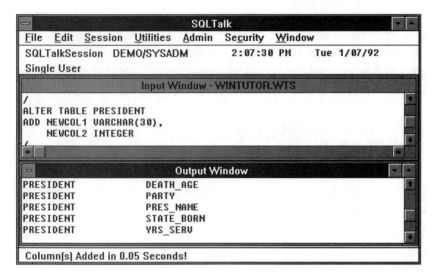

itself. As in the CREATE TABLE command, you can specify NULL, NOT NULL, or NULL WITH DEFAULT when you add or modify columns. Also, as with CREATE TABLE, the column names may be strung together, separated by commas as we show in our example. We are dropping a single column (sup_name) and adding two columns (sup_lname and sup_fname). Both are character data types and their lengths are 20 characters.

There are some special considerations for the use of the ALTER TABLE command. First, if you drop a column, any data in that column is lost. Second, you cannot change (modify) the data type of a column. You must drop it and add a new column with the new data type. Of course, any data in the dropped column is lost. Finally, you cannot drop a column that is the key for an index. As in just about any other command that affects tables, you cannot drop or modify columns in the data dictionary that were created by the system.

In all instances where you are adding a column, the syntax and optional clauses available are exactly the same as you use in the CREATE TABLE command. That includes the defaults in NOT NULL WITH DEFAULT, the column attributes, and the method of listing columns with commas. As you might expect, the commands in SQL that can become subcommands (as in a subselect) retain consistency in their syntax and options.

In the next chapter you will learn more about SQL commands. You will meet the most important of the SQL commands—the SELECT statement. SELECT is the most complex of all SQL commands, but it is the core of all SQL queries. You will also learn how to add, update, and delete data in your SQL tables.

QUICK SUMMARY

Here are some of the important points in this chapter. The word or phrase in bold lists a relational database feature. That feature's definition and its benefit to you follows.

Planning your database　Before you can begin seriously building your application you need to do a bit of planning, which starts with defining the tables you will include in your application's database.

Using CREATE　You use CREATE (object) when you want to build (define) the object from scratch.

CREATE DATABASE　CREATE DATABASE is a very simple command that has no additional keywords, predicates, or clauses. You use CREATE DATABASE to build a new database from scratch.

CREATE TABLE　CREATE TABLE and its accompanying clauses allow you to build a new table from scratch. You can define the table name and each of the columns in the table. You do not use CREATE TABLE to modify the structure of an SQL table.

CREATE INDEX　Use CREATE INDEX to build indexes for your tables. Indexes allow you to access information quickly because they define the reordering of the table based upon the contents of a specified column called the key. Index files do not physically reorder the table.

CREATE SYNONYM　A synonym is, really, no more than a shorthand method of referring to a table or view. Use the CREATE SYNONYM command to designate a synonym or "alias" for a table or view.

CREATE VIEW　A view is a virtual table created from one or more physical tables with only some of the data contained in the real tables. By a virtual table we mean that we won't create a real, physical table. Instead, we will set out the instructions to create such a table if we were going to do so.

DELETE and DROP DELETE DATABASE and DROP TABLE/VIEW/SYNONYM/INDEX are commands that allow you to delete the designated objects completely from your system.

ALTER TABLE ALTER TABLE allows you to add, delete, or modify the columns in a table. You can also rename columns or the table itself.

PRACTICE WHAT YOU'VE LEARNED

What You Should Do	How the Computer Responds
Start SQLBase and SQLTalk	SQL>
Type: ALTER TABLE test ADD phone char (14);	COLUMN(S) ADDED
SELECT * FROM test;	NAME AGE DOB PHONE ===================== peter 47 05-MAY-1944 1 ROW SELECTED
SELECT * FROM names;	NAME AGE DOB PHONE ===================== peter 47 05-MAY-1944 1 ROW SELECTED
CREATE VIEW birthday (name, birthday) AS SELECT name, dob FROM test;	VIEW CREATED
SELECT * FROM birthday;	NAME BIRTHDAY ================= peter 05-MAY-1944 1 ROW SELECTED
DROP TABLE test;	TABLE DROPPED

SELECT * FROM names;	Error: Table has not been created
SELECT * FROM birthday;	Error: Table has not been created

Querying and Updating Data

In Chapter 4 we looked at the elements you need to build an SQL query, including command line structure, statements, clauses, predicates, and subqueries. Now we'll begin to look at how you actually combine these elements to send commands to the database and have it return useful information. In Chapter 6 you will learn:

- ▲ **What the SELECT command does**
- ▲ **How to tailor a query**
- ▲ **How to add information**
- ▲ **How to revise information**
- ▲ **How to remove information**

SELECT

The basic method of choosing data, either for informational purposes or in preparation for modifying the database, is the SELECT command. By itself, it is much too vague to be of any practical use, since there's nothing in the command that lets the database know precisely what it is you're trying to call forth.

However, the database needs some type of attention-getting device to notify it that you want it to do something in particular. The word SELECT is that attention getter. It sets up a condition within the program that lets the database know you want to perform some particular kinds of actions. Subsidiary commands (clauses and predicates) that follow the word SELECT in your command line tell it precisely what to bring to the screen.

Once you construct a SELECT command with all of the information that tells the database program what you want it to do, the program delivers a product called a result table. The result table consists of the rows of data you specified by including those subsidiary clauses and predicates after the word SELECT in your command.

TIP

You have to have special authority to use the SELECT command. Database administrators assign SELECT privileges to individual users on a table-by-table or view-by-view basis.

When you've constructed a complete SELECT command that includes the clauses and predicates that tell the program what you want, SELECT will bring to your screen the data you specified, in the order (ascending or descending) you want it shown.

Adding Clauses and Predicates to SELECT

Figure 6.1 graphically describes the structure of a SELECT command.

▼ *Figure 6.1. SELECT Command Structure (Gupta Technologies)*

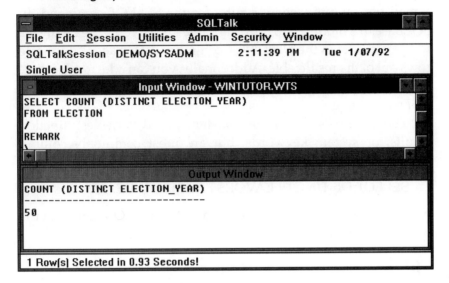

You begin building a SELECT command by first typing the word SELECT. You then proceed to tell the database what you want it to choose. You start by specifying whether you want to see the data from the entire table (ALL) or only data from specific rows. In SQLBase, ALL is the default, meaning that the entire table will be retrieved unless you specify otherwise. For example:

SELECT CUSTOMER;

is the same as

SELECT ALL CUSTOMER;

in that both commands will get you all of the rows in the CUS-TOMER table.

TIP

If you create LONG VARCHAR columns (columns where the value can be longer than 254 bytes) in SQLBase, you can only retrieve them with the ALL selection method.

UNIQUE

If you want to be more selective in the data you choose, you enter a modifier for uniqueness right after the SELECT command. In SQLBase this modifier goes by the name DISTINCT. (See Figure 6.2 for an example of the DISTINCT command.) This keeps duplicate rows out of the result table. Additionally, you can add a "select list" that consists of additional expressions to further modify the data you're choosing.

These expressions can be constants, bind variables, function results, or system keywords, but are most commonly column names from individual tables. For example:

SELECT DISTINCT FLAVORS FROM ICECREAM;

would make a list of just the nonduplicate flavors contained in the ICECREAM table.

FROM

You will have noticed that we introduced another SELECT clause in the example above, namely, the FROM clause. The FROM clause follows the select list. It is used to specify the names of the tables you're searching in order to create your result table.

▼ *Figure 6.2. Example of the DISTINCT command*

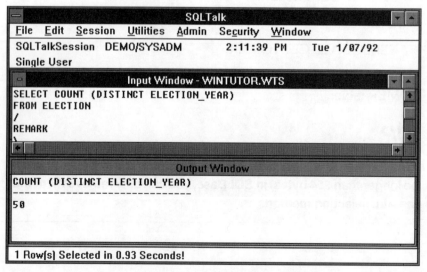

Wildcard SELECT

If you want the database program to deliver the information from a specific table, you can use an asterisk (*) to show all of the columns in that table. You can also use the asterisk to indicate that you want to see all of the columns in all of the tables you want to search. For example:

    SELECT ICECREAM.* ;

would tell the program to deliver a list of all of the columns in the ICECREAM table. This is just another way of saying: SELECT ALL ICECREAM; or SELECT ICECREAM;

However, if you write:

    SELECT *, ICECREAM, CANDY;

you get all of the columns in both tables.

If you decide to enter particular column names in the select list, each one must positively identify one (and only one) column in one table. In other words, each column-name must be unique. If columns have the same name in more than one table, you have to identify the column names according to which table they come from. For example:

    SELECT ICECREAM.FLAVORS,
    FROM ICECREAM, CANDY
    WHERE ICECREAM.FLAVORS = CANDY.FLAVORS;

CHECK YOURSELF

1. SELECT all of the columns in a database.

2. SELECT only the column FLAVORS in the ICECREAM database.

ANSWERS

1. Type SELECT [table-name]; where [table-name] is the name of the database you want to query.

2. Type SELECT ICECREAM.FLAVORS;

WHERE

The next way to modify a SELECT command is to include a WHERE clause (see Figure 6.3).

WHERE specifies a "search condition" or predicate that further refines how you want to choose the information to be displayed on the result table. Search conditions include the predicates BETWEEN, IN, LIKE, and EXISTS.

BETWEEN

BETWEEN compares a value with a range of values, for example:

    SELECT * FROM COMPUTERS
    WHERE PRICE BETWEEN 1000 AND 3000;

would give you a result table containing a list of computers (from the COMPUTERS table) having a price (from the PRICE column) of BETWEEN 1000 and 3000 dollars.

IN

IN compares a value to a collection of values, for example:

    SELECT * FROM COMPUTERS
    WHERE PRICE IN (1000,2000,3000);

▼ **Figure 6.3. WinTalk example of WHERE clause**

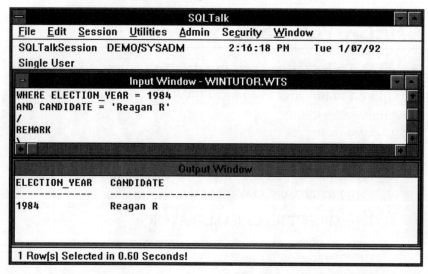

would select all computers from the COMPUTERS table that have prices that are 1000, 2000, and 3000 dollars. This is more precise than BETWEEN because you'll only get a match where the price of the computer is represented in whole thousands. More often, you'd want to use this predicate to make exact matches on names, dates, departments, colors, or anything where matching exact values is more important than finding a broad range of values.

LIKE

The LIKE predicate is used with the WHERE clause when you want to look for data that matches a particular pattern. The percent sign (%) and the underscore (_) are the pattern-matching characters. The % is like the DOS wildcard * and you use it to designate character strings of any length. You use the _ to designate a single character. For example:

```
SELECT * FROM TREES
WHERE NAME LIKE 'B%';
```

would search the TREES table and bring up any name starting with the letter B, like Birch, Beech, and Baobab. On the other hand, the command:

```
SELECT * FROM TREES
WHERE NAME LIKE 'B_ _ _ _';
```

would yield only Birch and Beech, since you specified an exact number of characters in the name.

EXISTS

The EXISTS predicate lets you know if a particular row (or rows) is present in a table; it returns True if the value exists. EXISTS has to be included in a query as part of a subquery called a subselect. For example, you can find all the members of a company department if you frame a query that looks like:

```
SELECT * FROM SALES
WHERE EXISTS (SELECT * FROM CUSTOMERS WHERE OR-
DERAMT = :1);
```

What you're doing is telling the DBMS to tell you of the existence of records in the SALES table, but only those records that have an order amount (ORDERAMT) in the CUSTOMERS table that is equal to the value of variable :1.

Variable :1 is a bind variable. A bind variable associates a syntactic location in an SQL command with a data value that is to be used in that command. The fact that it is :1 means that it is the first (Figure 6.4) (and, in this case, the only) variable in the statement. In a query such as this you could use a bind variable instead of a specific dollar amount as a way of setting up the query so that you can vary the dollar amount each time you run the search. If you later want to search for customers with whom you do a different volume of sales, all you have to do is change the definition of the bind variable to the new sales amount.

TIP

Putting a bind variable into a statement makes it interactive. When you execute the statement above, for example, the program will ask you to supply the value of :1 at the time of execution.

▼ *Figure 6.4. SQLTalk example of a statement using two bind variables*

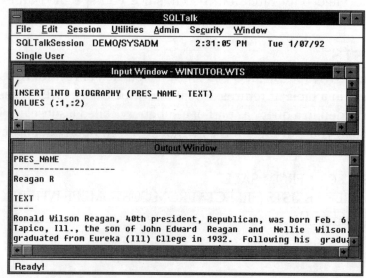

CHECK YOURSELF

Modify a SELECT command by including a WHERE clause.

ANSWER

Type SELECT [item] FROM [table-name]
WHERE [column-name] [search condition] [value]

Remember:

An item can be a column name, a constant, a bind variable, the result of a function, a system keyword, or another expression. The [table-name] is the database you want to search. WHERE notifies the DBMS that you only want to perform a specific kind of search for data located in a particular area (the [column-name]).

The [search condition] is the predicate (BETWEEN, IN, LIKE, or EXISTS) that modifies the WHERE clause and [value] is the thing you want the SELECT command to find.

GROUP BY

The GROUP BY clause modifies a SELECT command by organizing the result rows into sets according to the specific columns it names. You specify the columns you want to use as part of the GROUP BY clause. For example:

```
SELECT CUST.DEPTNO, DEPTNAME, SUM(SALES),
COUNT(CUSTNO)
FROM CUST, DEPT
WHERE CUST.DEPTNO = DEPT.DEPTNO
GROUP BY CUST.DEPTNO, DEPTNAME;
```

What you would get from the above statement is a list of rows in which all values of the grouping column will be equal. The list would show total sales and number of customers by each department. The statement WHERE CUST.DEPTNO = DEPT.DEPTNO is an example of an equijoin (which we'll get into next chapter) that we're using to derive the department names.

When you specify a GROUP BY clause, you have to make sure that the select list and the contents of the GROUP BY clause match.

Everything you list in GROUP BY also has to be contained in the select list.

TIP

The only exception to this rule that the SELECT list and the GROUP BY list have to match is when your SELECT list contains items that are aggregate set functions (like SUM(SALES), or COUNT(CUSTNO), above). Aggregate functions are not allowed as grouping columns since aggregate functions yield one value.

HAVING

The HAVING clause modifies the GROUP BY clause. HAVING contains its own set of search conditions that you use to refine the GROUP further (see Figure 6.5). For example, in the SELECT statement above, you could decide you only wanted to include departments with sales over $10,000. You would, therefore, add the HAVING clause right after the GROUP BY clause, like this:

    GROUP BY CUST.DEPTNO, DEPTNAME
    HAVING SUM(SALES) > 10000;

TIP

In order to be used in a HAVING clause, a grouping column must be an expression that is an aggregate function.

CHECK YOURSELF

Find the minimum and maximum sales for all flavors of ice cream.

ANSWER

Type:
SELECT FLAVOR, MIN(SALES), MAX(SALES)
FROM ICECREAM
GROUP BY FLAVOR;

▼ *Figure 6.5. A SQLTalk Windows HAVING clause example*

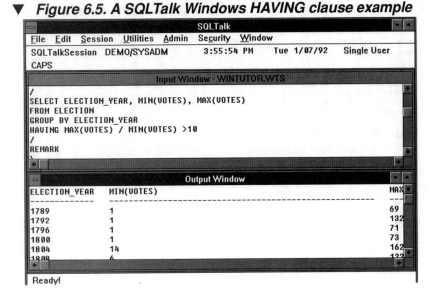

UNION

A UNION clause lets you combine the results of two or more queries (see Figure 6.6). It merges the results of query number one with the results of query number two, eliminating duplicate rows as it goes along. For example, if you wanted to find out which members of your marketing staff are engaged in working on the Quigley account, you would enter:

SELECT EMPNO FROM EMP WHERE DEPT = MKTDEPT
UNION
SELECT   EMPNO   FROM   ACCOUNT   WHERE
ACCOUNTNAME = QUIGLEY;

TIP

Each result table has to have the same number of columns and none of the columns can be of the **LONG VARCHAR** data type. Also, except for the column names, the description of the columns has to be the same from one table to the other.

▼ *Figure 6.6. Example of UNION from SQLTalk Windows*

```
┌─────────────────────────────────────────────────────────────────┐
│ ─                         SQLTalk                         ▼ ▲     │
│ File  Edit  Session  Utilities  Admin  Security  Window          │
│ SQLTalkSession  DEMO/SYSADM        4:11:32 PM   Tue 1/07/92   Single User │
│ CAPS                                                              │
│ ┌─────────────────── Input Window - WINTUTOR.WTS ────────── ▼ ▲  │
│ │popular vote and who were born in the state of Nebraska or Illinois.  This │
│ │involves a UNION of two queries, one on the WINNER table, and the other  on │
│ │the PRESIDENT table.                                             │
│ │/                                                                │
│ │SELECT NAME FROM WINNER                                          │
│ │UNION                                                            │
│ │SELECT PRES_NAME FROM PRESIDENT                                  │
│ │WHERE STATE_BORN IN ('Nebraska','Illinois')                     │
│ │/                                                                │
│ ├─────────────────────────────────────────────────────────────  │
│ │ELECTION_YEAR   CANDIDATE                                        │
│ │-------------   --------------------                             │
│ │1984            Reagan R                                         │
│ │1984            Reagan R                                         │
│ │                                                                 │
│ └─────────────────────────────────────────────────────────────  │
│ Ready!                                                            │
└─────────────────────────────────────────────────────────────────┘
```

In the text example above, the result of the UNION clause would be the employees from the marketing department engaged in this particular account. Other employees who might also be working on that account, such as those from sales, training, or finance, are not included in the UNION result table.

INSERT

Another command you'll often use in working with existing tables or views is called INSERT. Since adding new information to keep a database current is one of the principal activities in maintaining any kind of data, you'll be using this particular command a lot.

TIP

In many SQL databases, including SQLBase, users have to be specifically authorized, with INSERT privileges, before they can use this command.

To add a complete new row of data, type:

INSERT INTO [table-name or view-name] VALUES
(value,value,value);

What you're doing here is completely filling out a row, so all you have to do is list the value you want for each column. Values can be constants, bind variables, or system keywords.

If you only wanted to put a value in the first and third columns, but not the middle column, you would have to name the columns before you listed the values, such as:

INSERT INTO [table-name or view-name] [column-1,column-3] VALUES
(value,value);

The first value will be added to the first column listed and the second value will go into the third column. Since the middle column's name isn't included in the column-name list, it will be skipped.

TIP

When you list column values, be sure to separate them with a comma but do not use spaces before or after the comma.

You can also call new data into a table by drawing it out of a different table. In other words, you can "cut and paste" data from one table to another. You do this by using a subselect such as:

INSERT INTO NOVELS SELECT NAME FROM AUTHORS
WHERE STATUS = 'FICTION';

where:
NOVELS is the name of the target table; AUTHORS is the name of the source table; NAME designates value from the source table; and STATUS = 'FICTION' is the search condition you are using to perform your subselect.

What you have to remember when using a subselect, however, is that the source and target tables have to have the same number of columns and the rows you select have to match with regard to the data types and length of data.

TIP

Some SQL databases, including SQLBase, will convert the values of the source into values appropriate for the target if that is at all possible. For example, date/time values can be read into a numeric column, and vice versa. This can get you out of a jam from time to time but, for the most part, It's always best to try to match data types.

CHECK YOURSELF

1. Update a table by inserting a complete new row.

2. Update a table by inserting a partial row of data.

3. Update a table by drawing on information from another table.

ANSWERS

1. Type:
    INSERT INTO [table-name or view-name] VALUES (value,value,value)

    where:
    [table-name or view-name] is the name of the database you want to update; and

    (value,value,value) represents the data you are inputting.

2. Type:
    INSERT INTO [table-name or view-name] [column-1,column-2] VALUES (value,value)
    where:
    [table-name or view-name] is the name of the database you want to update; [column-1,column-2] represents the names of the columns to which you want to add information; and (value,value) represents the new data.

3. Type:
    INSERT INTO [target table] SELECT [value] FROM [source table]
    WHERE [subquery search condition];

UPDATE

UPDATE

The UPDATE command is in many ways similar to INSERT (see Figure 6.7). Both perform the task of adding new values to a table or view. However, while INSERT creates an entirely new row, UPDATE puts new values into columns and rows that already exist.

TIP

Like INSERT, UPDATE cannot be used unless the user has been granted specific permission to do so.

The form of an UPDATE command is:

UPDATE [table-name or view-name]
SET [column-name] = [expression] WHERE [search-condition];

You could use it for any kind of an update. For example, if you wanted to give 'SOMEBODY' an increased royalty, your UPDATE command would look like:

UPDATE AUTHORS SET ROYALTIES = ROYALTIES*1.5

▼ *Figure 6.7. SQLTalk UPDATE command example*

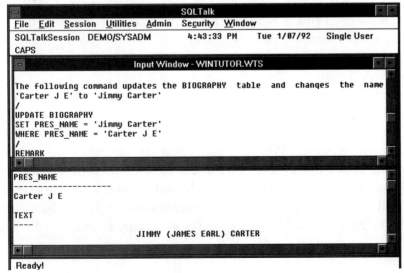

WHERE NAME = 'SOMEBODY';

AUTHORS is your table name; SET is the instruction to perform an update; ROYALTIES is the column-name whose value you want to change; the equal sign (=) indicates that you want to change the value of the expression in the column to something else; ROYAL-TIES*1.5 is the new value of the column and it means that you are multiplying the value of the ROYALTIES column by 1.5. However, you are only making this change in one place, namely, in the row where the value of the NAME column is 'SOMEBODY'. Such a splendid individual would then get a 50% increase in royalty rates.

There are several optional clauses you can add to the UPDATE command. For example, if your WHERE search condition involves a correlated subquery (which we'll cover in the next chapter) you use a "correlation name" along with the table name.

You would frame your command by typing:

UPDATE [table-name] [correlation-name]
SET [column-name] = [expression]
WHERE [search-condition includes a subquery to the column-name]

or

WHERE CURRENT OF [cursor-name]
CHECK EXISTS;

This correlation name is a temporary table-name (TEMP, for example) that you combine with the column-name (TEMP.column-name, for example). You use it to refer to the column when it appears more than once in the same UPDATE command as a way of avoiding ambiguity. It's an option and you only need it if the search condition involves a correlated subquery--something we'll learn more about in Chapter 7.

A second option is WHERE CURRENT OF cursor-name. You can use it in place of WHERE and it causes the update you specified in the SET clause to take place at the cursor's present location on the screen. If you're setting up a table where you want the user to scroll through a file and update information on a "spot" basis, the WHERE CURRENT OF cursor-name is the variant you should use.

However, before you can use the WHERE CURRENT OF cursor-name clause, you first have to assign a name to the current cursor.

Type:

SET CURSORNAME 'textstring';

In fact, you need to have two open cursors, so you would use the SET CURSORNAME command twice. The first cursor (for example, Cursor1) is associated with the SELECT command while the second cursor (for example, Cursor2) is associated with the UPDATE command. There's quite a bit more involved when you want to set up the database environment to allow line-by-line updating. We'll be covering that material when we get to Embedded SQL in Chapter 9.

Finally, you can add a CHECK EXISTS clause as the last statement in the command. It causes the program to display an error message if at least one row is not updated. CHECK EXISTS is particularly useful as an integrity check to make sure that all of your updates take place.

UPDATE

CHECK YOURSELF

Change the name of a FLAVOR from 'CHOCOLATE' to 'HOT FUDGE' in an ICECREAM database.

ANSWER

Type:
UPDATE ICECREAM SET FLAVOR = 'HOT FUDGE'
WHERE NAME = 'CHOCOLATE';

DELETE

The DELETE command lets you remove one or more rows from a single table or view. When you use it, all of the rows that meet the search conditions you specify in the WHERE clause are permanently removed from the table. If you use DELETE with a view, the specified rows are removed from the underlying table on which the view is built. To use DELETE, type:

DELETE FROM [table-name or view-name] [correlation-name (if required)]
WHERE [search-condition]

or

WHERE CURRENT OF [cursor-name]

For example, if you've decided that your experiment with turnip-flavored ice cream will not turn into a marketing success and want to delete it from the database, you would type:

DELETE FROM ICECREAM
WHERE FLAVOR = TURNIP

TIP

Users have to have DELETE privileges assigned before they can execute this command.

To let users scroll through a table and delete individual rows when the cursor comes to them, you would use the WHERE CURRENT OF cursor-name clause instead of the WHERE clause. However, before you can use the WHERE CURRENT OF cursor-name clause, you first have to assign a name to the current cursor.

Type:

SET CURSORNAME 'textstring';

In fact, you need to have two open cursors, so you would use the SET CURSORNAME command twice. The first cursor (for example, Cursor1) is associated with the SELECT command while the second cursor (for example, Cursor2) is associated with the DELETE command. There's quite a bit more involved when you want to set up the database environment to allow line-by-line deletions. We'll be covering that material when we get to Embedded SQL in Chapter 9.

QUICK SUMMARY

Here are some important points in this chapter. The word or phrase in bold lists a relational database feature. That feature's definition and its benefit to you follows.

SELECT This command finds, retrieves, and displays data. It specifies tables to be searched, search conditions, and the sequence in which data will be output.

ALL The ALL clause in the SELECT command is the default. You don't have to specify it. It automatically retrieves all of the rows in a table.

DISTINCT The DISTINCT clause in a SELECT command keeps the DBMS from displaying duplicate rows.

Select-list A select-list consists of expressions, usually column names, from one or more tables. When you use the SELECT command, the select-list is the group of rows you want to work with.

FROM The FROM clause in a SELECT command contains the names of the tables or views where the desired data can be found.

WHERE The WHERE clause sets up a "search condition," meaning that it prepares the DBMS to work with a PREDICATE. A PREDICATE, in turn, refines the search for information by telling the DBMS to bring you only such information as specified by the conditions BETWEEN, LIKE, IN, and EXISTS.

GROUP BY The GROUP BY clause in a SELECT command forms the result rows of a query into sets according to the column-names you choose to use with this clause.

HAVING The HAVING clause is used with its own search condition and is used with GROUP BY to further refine the way you want the results of your search displayed.

UNION The UNION clause of a SELECT command merges the result of two or more SELECTs.

INSERT The INSERT command adds new rows of data to a table or a view.

UPDATE The UPDATE command lets you change the value of one or more columns in a table or view and employs search conditions to make sure you only alter the specific columns you want to update.

DELETE The DELETE command removes rows from a table (or a view's base table) if they satisfy the requirements of a search condition.

PRACTICE WHAT YOU'VE LEARNED

1. SELECT all of the columns in a database.

2. SELECT only the column FLAVORS in the ICECREAM database.

3. Modify a SELECT command by including a WHERE clause.

4. Find the minimum and maximum sales for all flavors of ice cream.

5. Update a table by inserting a complete new row.

6. Update a table by inserting a partial row of data.

7. Update a table by drawing on information from another table.

8. Change the name of a FLAVOR from 'CHOCOLATE' to 'HOT FUDGE' in an ICECREAM database.

ANSWERS

1. Type:
   SELECT [table-name]; where [table-name] is the name of the database you want to query.

2. Type:
   SELECT ICECREAM.FLAVORS;

3. Type:
   SELECT [item] FROM [table-name]
   WHERE [column-name] [search condition] [value]

4. Type:
   SELECT FLAVOR, MIN(SALES), MAX(SALES)
   FROM ICECREAM
   GROUP BY FLAVOR;

5. Type:
   INSERT INTO [table-name or view-name] VALUES
   (value,value,value)
   where:
   [table-name or view-name] is the name of the database you
   want to update; and
   (value,value,value) represents the data you are inputting.

6. Type:
   INSERT INTO [table-name or view-name] [column-1,col-
   umn-2] VALUES
   (value,value)
   where:

   [table-name or view-name] is the name of the database you
   want to update; [column-1,column-2] represents the names
   of the columns to which you want to add information; and
   (value,value) represents the new data.

7. Type:
   INSERT INTO [target table] SELECT [value] FROM [source
   table]
   WHERE [subquery search condition];

8. Type:
   UPDATE ICECREAM SET FLAVOR = 'HOT FUDGE'
   WHERE NAME = 'CHOCOLATE';

Complex Queries

In the last chapter you learned the basics of using SQL to query and update tables. In this chapter you'll discover that the capabilities of SQL are very much greater than the rudiments we've discussed so far. Beginning now, we'll go into the details of querying tables to generate various combinations of data in our final output. The basic SQL tools for performing complex queries are the join and the subquery. Our exploration will center on using joins and subqueries in:

- ▲ **Single tables**
- ▲ **Two or more tables**
- ▲ **Multiple tables**
- ▲ **Subqueries with a single value**
- ▲ **Correlated subqueries**
- ▲ **Multiple nested subqueries**

Because you can sometimes get caught up in creating complexity for its own sake—and that tends to spin off into sometimes fascinating, but often limited, technical virtuosity—we'll try to stick to fundamental concepts. As you develop your own familiarity with the primary techniques of complex queries, you'll quickly see ways to expand you own uses for the techniques we've described.

Using Joins

The basic definition of a "join" is the practice of pulling data for a single result from two or more tables. You set up a search condition in which you tell the DBMS that the information you want is the result of data that resides in two or more separate tables. The program then goes out to those individual tables, finds the specific data you want from each one, and presents you with a new set of data that shows the previously separated information "joined" in a new relationship.

Single Table

While all of the above is true, it overlooks one of the most commonly used functions of a join, which is to present data from the same table in new, unique, or specific ways.

Self-Joins

Starting out with a single table, for example a database of employees, you use a self-join to help you sift through masses of raw data and find the specific correlations that can give you the information you want—without all the rest of the data that in this instance would just get in the way.

If you wanted to search the above-mentioned employees database to find all of the people hired on the same day you were hired, for example, you could perform a self-join by typing:

```
SELECT EMP2.NAME, EMP2.HIRE_DATE
FROM EMPLOYEES EMP1, EMPLOYEES EMP2
WHERE EMP1.HIRE_DATE=EMP2.HIRE_DATE
AND EMP1.NAME = '[your name]'
```

You give the EMPLOYEES table two fictional "correlation names" so that it now appears to the program as though it were two different tables. You retrieve the date you were hired from correlation table EMP1 and use it as the condition for searching correlation table EMP2.

What you get is a result set that ignores everything in the EMPLOYEES table except a list of names, including yours, where everybody listed was hired the same day you were. You can do the same thing by using a subquery. We'll cover that a little later in the chapter.

CHECK YOURSELF

Use a self-join to find all the customers in a table who have the same ZIP code as the location of your biggest customer.

ANSWER

Type:
```
SELECT CUST2.NAME, CUST2.ZIP_CODE
FROM CUSTOMERS CUST1, CUSTOMERS CUST2
WHERE CUST1.ZIP_CODE=CUST2.ZIP_CODE
AND CUST1.NAME = '[biggest customer]';
```

Two or More Tables

While joins in a single table are helpful, the main function of a join is really to help you combine information from completely different tables in a way that hands you new information (see Figure 7.1). The ability to compare different tables and draw from them unsuspected correlations, or derive results that might take hour or days to come up with manually, is really what the power of SQL is all about.

▼ *Figure 7.1. An example of a multiple-table JOIN*

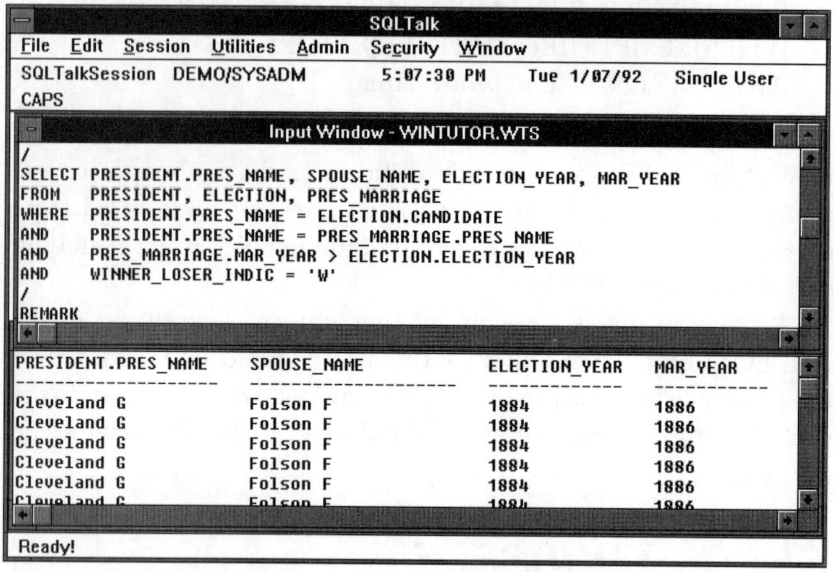

```
┌─────────────────────────────────────────────────────────────────────┐
│ ─                            SQLTalk                          ▼  ▲   │
├─────────────────────────────────────────────────────────────────────┤
│ File  Edit  Session  Utilities  Admin  Security  Window            │
├─────────────────────────────────────────────────────────────────────┤
│ SQLTalkSession  DEMO/SYSADM        5:07:30 PM    Tue 1/07/92   Single User │
│ CAPS                                                                │
│ ┌─────────────────────────────────────────────────────────────────┐ │
│ │ ─              Input Window - WINTUTOR.WTS            ▼  ▲        │ │
│ ├─────────────────────────────────────────────────────────────────┤ │
│ │/                                                                 │ │
│ │SELECT PRESIDENT.PRES_NAME, SPOUSE_NAME, ELECTION_YEAR, MAR_YEAR  │ │
│ │FROM    PRESIDENT, ELECTION, PRES_MARRIAGE                        │ │
│ │WHERE   PRESIDENT.PRES_NAME = ELECTION.CANDIDATE                  │ │
│ │AND     PRESIDENT.PRES_NAME = PRES_MARRIAGE.PRES_NAME             │ │
│ │AND     PRES_MARRIAGE.MAR_YEAR > ELECTION.ELECTION_YEAR           │ │
│ │AND     WINNER_LOSER_INDIC = 'W'                                  │ │
│ │/                                                                 │ │
│ │REMARK                                                            │ │
│ ├─────────────────────────────────────────────────────────────────┤ │
│ │PRESIDENT.PRES_NAME      SPOUSE_NAME           ELECTION_YEAR   MAR_YEAR │ │
│ │-------------------      -------------------   -------------   ---------- │ │
│ │Cleveland G              Folson F              1884          1886  │ │
│ │Cleveland G              Folson F              1884          1886  │ │
│ │Cleveland G              Folson F              1884          1886  │ │
│ │Cleveland G              Folson F              1884          1886  │ │
│ │Cleveland G              Folson F              1884          1886  │ │
│ │Cleveland G              Folson F              1884          1886  │ │
│ └─────────────────────────────────────────────────────────────────┘ │
│ Ready!                                                              │
└─────────────────────────────────────────────────────────────────────┘
```

In the example showing a single-table join, you'll have noticed that we actually fooled the program into thinking it was dealing with two tables by creating correlation names. When you work with at least two different tables you don't have to indulge in such a ruse. On the other hand, in a single-table join you don't have to worry about matching primary keys while multiple-table joins are impossible unless there is some column of common data you can use as your primary key.

Cartesian Product

You also have to be careful not to specify your search condition too loosely when you're calling for information from more than one table. Unless you specify your search condition as a relational predicate, you'll wind up with what's called a Cartesian product. A Cartesian product is the set of all possible rows resulting from a join in both tables. For example, asking for the join:

SELECT SUPPLIER.NAME, INVOICENO FROM SUPPLIERS, INVOICES;

would yield every possible combination of rows in the SUPPLIERS table and the INVOICE table. If you deal with ten different suppliers and have 20 invoices, your result table would have 200 rows. The way you really want to structure your query is:

Using Joins

    SELECT SUPPLIER.NAME, INVOICENO
    FROM SUPPLIERS, INVOICES
    WHERE SUPPLIER.SUPPLIERNO = INVOICE.SUPPLIERNO;

This way, you get each supplier and invoice listed in a result table containing 20 rows. If one supplier has sent you six invoices, you would get six rows following that name.

TIP

The program will still generate a Cartesian product but it then performs the extra step of eliminating all of the rows that fail to meet the join condition.

Equijoin

What's demonstrated by the second example, above, is called an equijoin. The result table with the supplier row containing the supplier's name and number is "joined" to each of the invoice rows that also contain the supplier's number. The SUPPLIERNO column is the key that relates both tables.

The type of join is called an equijoin because it is based on an "equality" that exists between both tables, that is, the SUPPLIERNO column.

CHECK YOURSELF

Create a result table matching the correct model airplane parts with the proper model airplane kit.

ANSWER

Type:
SELECT KIT.NAME, PARTNO
FROM KITS, PARTS
WHERE KIT.KITNO = PART.KITNO;

Non-Equijoin

As we mentioned, an equijoin is based on an "equality" between two or more tables. You can also make comparisons between tables based on any other relational operator (>, <, !=, BETWEEN, and LIKE). This kind of comparison is called a non-equijoin.

TIP

Non-equijoins are also referred to as "Theta Joins." Regardless of what they are called, they are joins that use relational operators to define the join condition.

You could use the BETWEEN operator, for example, to find out if your model airplane kits in the previous CHECK YOURSELF example each contain the correct number of parts. You can check this by looking at the recorded weight of each package you ship.

You would have, for example, a KITS table containing the minimum and maximum permitted weight for each kit, perhaps allowing for variations in the thickness of pieces within a tolerance range. Each kit has an individual shipping number and the weight of each kit is recorded as it leaves the production area.

```
SELECT MODEL_NAME, KITS.SHIPNO, WEIGHT
FROM KITS, WEIGHTS
WHERE KITS.SHIPNO = WEIGHT.PRODUCTNO
AND WEIGHT NOT BETWEEN TOOLIGHT AND
TOOHEAVY;
```

In this situation you would wind up with a listing of model names and numbers that were shipped either overweight or underweight, possibly pointing to inconsistencies in materials or packaging quality control.

CHECK YOURSELF

Use a non-equijoin to discover if any employee's salary falls below or above the minimum and maximum set for their grade level by finding any rows outside that range.

ANSWER

Set up a search of the EMPLOYEES table and the PAY_LEVELS table:
SELECT NAME, EMPLOYEE.GRADE, PAY
FROM EMPLOYEES, PAY_LEVELS
WHERE EMPLOYEE.GRADE = PAY.GRADE
AND PAY NOT BETWEEN MINPAY AND MAXPAY;

Outer Join

One of the characteristics of equijoins and non-equijoins is that they omit rows when entries in one or another of the columns don't meet the search conditions. Most of the time, this is exactly what you want.

There are times, however, when you want all of the rows present. For example, in the equijoin above, we developed a list of only those suppliers who'd sent invoices.

If we wanted, instead, to list all suppliers with an eye toward finding out which ones had not yet sent an invoice, we could perform what's called an outer join. An outer join forces a row from one (and only one) of the tables to appear in the result if no match is found. This will give us the names of even those suppliers who have sent us what we ordered but haven't yet sent us a bill.

To do this, we'd modify the equijoin by instead typing:

SELECT SUPPLIER.SUPPLIERNO, NAME
FROM SUPPLIERS, INVOICES
WHERE SUPPLIER.SUPPLIERNO =
INVOICE.SUPPLIERNO(+);

The plus sign (+) tells the program to create another row. This new row contains all the Null values that will be temporarily added to the INVOICES table. The program then joins the Null row of the INVOICES table to rows in the SUPPLIERS table that have no matching invoices. The result, as we want, will be all suppliers, whether or not they have sent an invoice.

TIP

Only one-way outer joins can be performed. You cannot use the plus sign on both names.

If we decide next that we want a table containing only those suppliers who haven't yet billed us, we can search just for the Null rows we created above.

SELECT SUPPNAME, SUPPLIER.NAME
FROM SUPPLIERS, INVOICES
WHERE SUPPLIER.SUPPLIERNO =
INVOICE.SUPPLIERNO(+)
AND INVOICE.SUPPLIERNO IS NULL;

CHECK YOURSELF

1. Use an outer join to find employees and how much vacation time they've taken this year, including employees who have not taken their vacations yet.

2. List only those employees who have not taken any vacation time.

ANSWERS

1. Select your data from the EMPLOYEES table and the SCHEDULING table by typing:
   SELECT EMPLOYEE.VACATIONS, EMPNAME
   FROM EMPLOYEES, SCHEDULING
   WHERE EMPLOYEE.EMPNAME = SCHEDULING.VA-CATION_DAYS(+);

2. Search for only the Null row matches by typing:
   SELECT EMPLOYEE.VACATIONS, EMPNAME
   FROM EMPLOYEES, SCHEDULING
   WHERE EMPLOYEE.EMPNAME = SCHEDULING.VA-CATION_DAYS
   AND SCHEDULING.VACATION_DAYS IS NULL;

Using Subqueries

A subquery is a search condition within another search condition (see Figure 7.2). It specifies a result table from one or more tables or views in the same way as any other search condition. A subquery is different from a normal query in that each of its result rows is used to narrow down the list of search conditions for the main, or outer, search condition.

TIP

Subqueries are also known as "nested SELECTs," nested queries, and "subselects." Regardless of the name, they apply to SELECT statements that reside within other SELECT statements.

You can have relatively straightforward, single-value subqueries or successively complex "correlated subqueries" and "multiple nested subqueries." You'll notice that subqueries perform much the same function as a self-join and in many cases the two forms of search mode can be used interchangeably.

▼ **Figure 7.2. Another example of a nested SELECT command**

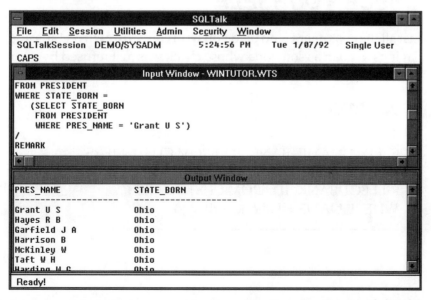

Subselects of the first type, the single-value subquery, help us find information hidden in a table. They bring out data and highlight it by presenting that information in isolation. For example, you might be able to get an idea of what percentage of your work force is going to retire when you do by matching the hiring dates of everybody who became an employee with the company at the same time as you.

You would set up a single-value subquery by typing:

SELECT NAME, HIRE_DATE FROM EMPLOYEES
WHERE HIRE_DATE =
(SELECT HIRE_DATE FROM EMPLOYEES
WHERE NAME = ['my name'];)

The SQL program first finds the date you were hired. Then it uses this value to compare against every other name and hire date in the employee database.

What you wind up with is a list of people who were all hired at the same time as you and, all else being equal, may very well leave the work force at the same time. Even if you find the information to be of value only for curiosity's sake, you can see how you could apply this search structure to other, more relevant, information. For example, you could find all the products manufactured on the same day as a product with a known materials defect.

CHECK YOURSELF

List all the customers who paid you with checks drawn on the same Savings & Loan as someone whose check was just refused by your bank.

ANSWER

Type:
SELECT NAME, BANK_ID, FROM CUSTOMERS
WHERE BANK_ID =
(SELECT BANK_ID FROM CUSTOMERS
WHERE NAME = ['check_writer'];)

Correlated Subquery

A simple, or single-value, subquery like the one above executes once to retrieve a particular value, which is then used by the main query. We can also execute a subquery repetitively. Called a "correlated subquery," this type of search executes once for each candidate row in the main query (see Figure 7.3). For example, we could find the stocks whose selling price is higher than the New York Stock Exchange average on a given day by performing a search such as:

```
SELECT STOCK, PRICE
FROM STOCKS S
WHERE PRICE>
(SELECT AVG(PRICE) FROM STOCKS
WHERE S.PRICE = PRICE);
```

This search goes through a table of listed stocks and compares the price of each to the average price paid for a share of stock. The search goes through the stocks list once for each stock on the list.

You'll notice that we're using correlation names. This is because we're executing the search condition more than once for the same

▼ *Figure 7.3. Example of a correlated subquery*

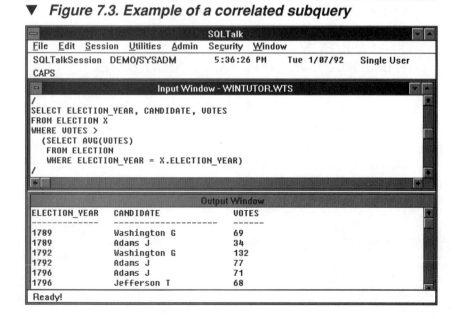

table in order to come up with a list of high-performing stocks. SQL requires that correlation names be used when you search a single table more than once.

TIP

The primary benefit of correlation names is that they help to eliminate the possible ambiguity of referring to a column name. Even if you might not get confused, the program would.

CHECK YOURSELF

Write a correlated subquery that requests the names of those paintings at each of an art gallery's auctions that were sold for more than the average amount received for the other paintings sold at the same time.

ANSWER

In a database with the names of paintings, dates of auctions, and amounts paid for each piece, you would type:

```
SELECT AUCTION_DATE, PAINTING, AMOUNT
FROM AUCTION X
WHERE AMOUNT>
(SELECT AVG(AMOUNT)
FROM AUCTION
WHERE AUCTION_DATE = X.AUCTION_DATE);
```

As a correlated subquery, the inner query will be executed once for each row of the outer query. Those paintings that fetched a higher than average price will be drawn into a separate table where just the dates they were sold, their names, and the amount they earned will be listed.

Multiple Nested Subqueries

Multiple nested subqueries are compositions of either or both single-value and/or correlated subqueries. Once you get comfortable using subqueries in the more straightforward forms listed above, you'll find that you can also use them to derive increasingly useful result tables from the information in your database.

For example, nested subqueries can be used with the IN predicate to compare a value to a collection of values returned from the inner query. The following example requests the names of those companies in a table of BANKS that were chartered in any of the same states as Silverado Savings and Loan or BCCI, Inc. The table was set up to include a one character code indicating whether the bank is now solvent or insolvent.

```
SELECT COMPANY_NAME, STATE_CHARTERED
FROM BANKS
WHERE STATE_CHARTERED IN
  (SELECT STATE_CHARTERED
  FROM BANKS
  WHERE COMPANY_NAME IN ('SILVERADO', 'BCCI')
    AND SOLVENT_INSOLVENT_INDIC = I);
```

CHECK YOURSELF

Find the order information on all sales made on the same day as a sale to company ABC.

ANSWERS

```
Connect to the ORDERS table and type:
SELECT * FROM ORDERS
WHERE ORDERDATE IN
(SELECT ORDERDATE FROM ORDERS
WHERE CUSTOMER = ABC);
```

With the INSERT Predicate

You can also use nested queries to pick rows from one table and insert them into another. For example, you could create a temporary table called BAILOUT that has three columns: the bank's NAME, the YEAR it went into federal receivership, and the number of DEPOSITORS who are being compensated by the Federal Deposit Insurance Corporation. The INSERT statement following the table's creation causes the names of all the companies from the BANKS table who have a SOLVENT_INSOLVENT_INDIC of I to be inserted into the BAILOUT table.

```
CREATE TABLE BAILOUT (NAME CHAR(20), YEAR
SMALLINT, DEPOSITORS SMALLINT);
    INSERT INTO BAILOUT
    SELECT NAME, YEAR, DEPOSITORS
    FROM BANKS
    WHERE SOLVENT_INSOLVENT_INDIC = 'I';
```

CHECK YOURSELF

Use a subquery to derive the rows you want to insert into another table.

ANSWER

In a table of model airplane kits, type:
INSERT INTO BIPLANES
SELECT KITNO, STYLE
FROM AIRPLANES
(SELECT WING_TYPE FROM AIRPLANES
WHERE STYLE = 'BP');

With the UNION Clause

Sometimes it is useful to query several tables and merge the rows that are returned into one set of results. This merging is called a UNION and a special operator exists in SQL to accomplish it. In the following query, we request to see the names of all automobiles that were recalled and that were manufactured in Sweden or France. This involves a UNION of two queries, one on the RECALL table and one on the AUTOMOBILES table, with a subquery on the IMPORTS table.

> SELECT NAME FROM RECALL
> UNION
> SELECT NAME FROM AUTOMOBILES
> WHERE ORIGIN IN
> (SELECT ORIGIN FROM IMPORTS
> WHERE COUNTRY = 'Sweden','France');

The above query will display all of the recalled cars that were imported from either Sweden or France.

TIP

In order to use the UNION clause, you have to make sure that both main queries have the same number of columns in the select list and that they have identical data types.

CHECK YOURSELF

Create a UNION that names the employees from the construction department who became ill while building a particular waste treatment plant.

ANSWER

> In a table of employees, type:
> SELECT NAME FROM EMP
> WHERE SICK_DAYS =
> (SELECT SICK_DAYS FROM EMP
> WHERE DEPT = CONSTRUCTION
> UNION
> SELECT PROJECT FROM PLANTS
> WHERE PROJECT = WASTE_TREATMENT;)

QUICK SUMMARY

Here are some of the important points in this chapter. The word or phrase in bold lists a relational database feature. That feature's definition and its benefit to you follows.

Join   A join is the practice of pulling data for a single result from two or more tables.

Single Table   In a single table, you can join that table to itself in an operation known as a self-join. You assign correlation names to the table and use them to qualify the column names in the rest of the query.

Cartesian product   In a join, the total of all possible combinations of all of the rows in all of the tables. By itself, this is an undesirable result. To get useful information you have to specify the search condition to eliminate the rows that do not meet the desired criteria.

Equijoin   A join where columns are compared on the basis of equality (the = symbol is used).

Non-equijoin   A join where columns are compared on the basis of relational operators (<, >, !=, BETWEEN, or LIKE).

Outer Join   A join in which rows are returned in the result table even if they contain Null values. It enables a join to include both matching and nonmatching rows.

Subquery   A SELECT command contained within the WHERE or HAVING clause of another SELECT command.

Correlated subquery   A subquery that is executed once for each row selected by the outer query.

Multiple nested subquery   Combinations of subqueries all residing with the same overall query that work to produce highly selective results from the original table or tables.

PRACTICE WHAT YOU'VE LEARNED

1. Use a self-join to find all the customers in a table who have the same ZIP code as the location of your biggest customer.

2. Create a result table matching the correct model airplane parts with the proper model airplane kit.

3. Use a non-equijoin to discover if any employee's salary falls below or above the minimum and maximum set for his or her grade level by finding any rows outside that range.

4. Use an outer join to find employees and how much vacation time they've taken this year, including employees who have not taken their vacations yet.

5. List only those employees who have not taken any vacation time.

6. List all the customers who paid you with checks drawn on the same Savings & Loan as someone whose check was just refused by your bank.

7. Write a correlated subquery that requests the names of those paintings at each of an art gallery's auctions that were sold for more than the average amount received for the other paintings sold at the same time.

8. Find the order information on all sales made on the same day as a sale to company ABC.

9. Use a subquery to derive the rows you want to insert into another table.

10. Create a UNION that names the employees from the construction department who became ill while building a particular waste treatment plant.

ANSWERS

1. Type:
    SELECT CUST2.NAME, CUST2.ZIP_CODE
    FROM CUSTOMERS CUST1, CUSTOMERS CUST2
    WHERE CUST1.ZIP_CODE=CUST2.ZIP_CODE
    AND CUST1.NAME = '[biggest customer]';

2. Type:
   SELECT KIT.NAME, PARTNO
   FROM KITS, PARTS
   WHERE KIT.KITNO = PART.KITNO;

3. Set up a search of the EMPLOYEES table and the PAY_LEV-ELS table:
   SELECT NAME, EMPLOYEE.GRADE, PAY
   FROM EMPLOYEES, PAY_LEVELS
   WHERE EMPLOYEE.GRADE = PAY.GRADE
   AND PAY NOT BETWEEN MINPAY AND MAXPAY;

4. Select your data from the EMPLOYEES table and the SCHEDULING table by typing:
   SELECT EMPLOYEE.VACATIONS, EMPNAME
   FROM EMPLOYEES, SCHEDULING
   WHERE EMPLOYEE.EMPNAME = SCHEDULING.VA-CATION_DAYS(+);

5. Search for only the Null row matches by typing:
   SELECT EMPLOYEE.VACATIONS, EMPNAME
   FROM EMPLOYEES, SCHEDULING
   WHERE EMPLOYEE.EMPNAME = SCHEDULING.VA-CATION_DAYS
   AND SCHEDULING.VACATION_DAYS IS NULL;

6. Type:
   SELECT NAME, BANK_ID, FROM CUSTOMERS
   WHERE BANK_ID =
   (SELECT BANK_ID FROM CUSTOMERS
   WHERE NAME = ['check_writer'];

7. In a database with the names of paintings, dates of auctions, and amounts paid for each piece, you could type:
   SELECT AUCTION_DATE, PAINTING, AMOUNT
   FROM AUCTION X
   WHERE AMOUNT>
   (SELECT AVG(AMOUNT)
   FROM AUCTION
   WHERE AUCTION_DATE = X.AUCTION_DATE);

8. Connect to the ORDERS table and type:
   SELECT * FROM ORDERS
   WHERE ORDERDATE IN
   (SELECT ORDERDATE FROM ORDERS
   WHERE CUSTOMER = ABC);

9. In a table of model airplane kits, type:
   INSERT INTO BIPLANES
   SELECT KITNO, STYLE
   FROM AIRPLANES
   (SELECT WING_TYPE FROM AIRPLANES
   WHERE STYLE = 'BP');

10. In a table of employees, type:
    SELECT NAME FROM EMP
    WHERE SICK_DAYS =
    (SELECT SICK_DAYS FROM EMP
    WHERE DEPT = CONSTRUCTION
    UNION
    SELECT PROJECT FROM PLANTS
    WHERE PROJECT = WASTE_TREATMENT;

Database
Security

Now that we've given some attention to the basics of creating and searching with SQL we need to stop a moment and take stock. Databases are extremely sensitive resources. Depending on the kind of information you need to store, your databases can be vital components of the way you run your business. By the same token, the more valuable the database becomes to you, the more important it is to make sure the information is immune from tampering, unauthorized editing, or even viewing by individuals with no need or right to do so.

In this chapter, we'll discuss:

- ▲ **The need for security**
- ▲ **The database administrator's role**
- ▲ **GRANT and REVOKE**
- ▲ **ALTER PASSWORD**

The Need for Database Security

As we mentioned above, the need for database security stems from the relative importance or sensitivity of the information you collect. For the most part, security is always going to be a high priority. If the information wasn't important or useful, you wouldn't be going to all the trouble of collecting it and formatting it in the first place.

What may not be so immediately apparent, however, is that the ability of SQL to combine seemingly unrelated bits of data into new, possibly unlooked-for relationships makes raw information potentially a much more valuable resource than ever before. This is the power of a structured query language. It turns data into information. As a result, database security is a prominent part of what a database's usefulness is all about. What you have to try to do is make sure that the valuable commodity known as information doesn't become the common property of those who are merely curious or actively hostile, as opposed to those who have a legitimate use for the information.

To take an obvious example, a pharmacist's database of patient medication can provide information that will keep people from taking drugs that, in combination with other drugs, could kill them. That same information in the hands of anyone else, however, is totally unwarranted. Any kind of information can be stored in a table. Whether it is your "business" to monitor stock market quotes or to keep records of phone calls at a crisis intervention center, there is always going to be some information that simply does not belong in the public domain.

The more detailed the information—and SQL lets you keep very detailed data indeed—the more important it is that the information be protected from unauthorized access. Since the question quickly passes from "why" you need security to "how" you go about obtaining it, let's move on to some specifics.

The Database Administrator's Role

The Database Administrator's Role

The primary mechanism for security in SQL databases revolves around a system of passwords, permissions, and rights. Just as your local area network is protected from intruders by the way you use these tools, so too is your database application. SQL also has a built-in mechanism that is part of the language, called the GRANT command. Additionally, most implementations of SQL contain a basic extension called the REVOKE command. Used in combination, GRANT and REVOKE let you give or take away an individual user's right to access information.

GRANT and REVOKE will be discussed more fully later in this chapter. For now, let's back up a little. There are actually two very powerful system personae in the SQL database environment. One is the system administrator (usually identified as SYSADM, or SA, or something similar) and the database administrator (usually identified as the DBA, or similar). Since we are using SQLBase as our model of how an SQL database environment is structured, we'll use examples specific to that package. However, most SQL database management systems will have structures very closely analogous to the examples we list.

The system administrator is the most powerful database authority. As SYSADM, you are the only person who can add new users. You can see anyone else's password and can change user passwords. You also are in charge of assigning authority levels to all other users.

TIP

A user cannot be granted SYSADM authority. You can't change the SYSADM user name (although you can change the SYSADM password) and you can have only one SYSADM for each database.

Just below the SYSADM is the database administrator (DBA). The DBA has all the same privileges as the SYSADM except for the authority to create new users, change passwords, or change their authority levels.

Below the DBA are two user levels. In SQLBase these user levels are called RESOURCE and CONNECT. A user with RESOURCE authority can create new tables. A user with CONNECT authority can access tables but cannot create them.

CHECK YOURSELF

1. What are the four levels of SQL users?

2. What are the authority levels for each?

ANSWERS

1. The four levels include the system administrator (SYS-ADM), database administrator (DBA), users with the authority to create new tables (RESOURCE), and users with access authority only (CONNECT).

2. The SYSADM has the highest level of authority and can create new users, assign authority levels, and change passwords; the DBA has all privileges on all tables and can assign or modify privileges for other users; the RESOURCE user can create and drop tables and assign privileges for other users in those tables; the CONNECT user has access authority, but only when specifically granted.

SYSADM

The SYSADM is the database superuser. It is the only persona that does not need special permission to access information anywhere in the system. In most SQL database management systems the SYSADM persona is an automatic construct. It is part of the package and is necessary for creating new users.

There is no initial password for the system administrator in most SQL implementations, so if you're installing an SQL DBMS for the first time, creating a password for the SYSADM will be one of the first things you'll want to do.

TIP

Procedures for setting up a SYSADM password vary with the particular implementation you're using, but this is key—tightly control access to the SYSADM password.

At first, the SYSADM is the only one allowed to create a database. This authority, as well as the authority to create lower-level privileges, can be transferred to other individuals after initial setup. Other authorities, such as creating new users or changing a user's authority level or password, are not transferable.

DBA

The step immediately below the SYSADM is the database administrator. It is at this level that most of the day-to-day operational functions of database management are conducted. Once granted the authority to create databases, DBAs have little recourse to the overriding authority of the SYSADM. In systems where the SYSADM and the DBA are the same person, you'll find that you'll rarely need to assume your SYSADM role while you'll be almost constantly active as a DBA. As a DBA, you are responsible for designing, planning, installing, configuring, securing, managing, maintaining, and operating the database management system. Depending on your organization, and whether or not you are both the SYSADM and the DBA your specific duties will include some or all of the following:

1. Daily maintenance
2. Diagnostics and system troubleshooting
3. Creating databases
4. Adding users to databases
5. Performing system backup and recovery
6. Assigning permissions levels to regular users
7. Installing client programs
8. Managing disk space and estimating storage needs
9. Fine-tuning database performance
10. Auditing database use
11. Advising and training users

12. Administering system catalogs
13. Ensuring the accuracy and integrity of data
14. Managing communications
15. Installing server programs and support files

For the most part, these are the DBA's jobs simply because lower-level users don't have the authority or training to handle them. The task of adding users is included in the list above even though it is a SYSADM function, because the person with SYSADM authority is usually also a DBA.

TIP

The SYSADM can function as a DBA because the organization of permission levels is hierarchical. The reverse (a DBA operating as a SYSADM) is not possible. You can go from a higher level to a lower one without being given specific authorization, but not the other way around.

The DBA usually runs the show on a day-to-day basis and generally will be the person most familiar with the DBMS and its workings. The DBA has all privileges on all objects (tables and views). There can be as many people with DBA privileges as the SYSADM wants to create and, depending on the size of your organization and the way you structure responsibilities, the DBA(s) may all perform each DBA task or each DBA may be responsible for only a few tasks out of the total list.

Regardless of how your organization is structured, however, the DBA will always have the potential to perform all of the tasks listed above, with the exception of creating new users, changing passwords, and changing authority levels for other users. The same potential does not come with lower-level privileges (RESOURCE and CONNECT).

GRANT

SQL databases are exclusive by nature. This is the primary level of security. To get started using any SQL database, a user must be given special permission to do so. Further, whatever authority levels the users have are the result of explicit commands issued by the SYSADM. The ability to add, delete, or modify information at any level is always the result of the user getting explicit permission to do so. The command that activates new users and gives them particular levels of authority is called the GRANT command. The command that takes away a user's authority at any level is the REVOKE command.

GRANT

The act of creating a new user is the SYSADM's responsibility and you do it by using a special form of the GRANT command. In SQLBase, this command looks like the following:

GRANT CONNECT TO [user-name] IDENTIFIED BY [password];

Regardless of whether or not you want to give this particular user greater authority (RESOURCE or DBA), you must always start out by GRANTing CONNECT authority and assigning a password. In some DBMS packages, and SQLBase is one of them, a password is mandatory for all new users.

The permissions level that comes along with the CONNECT authority lets the user log on to the database, use the SELECT command to query specifically authorized tables and views, use the INSERT, UPDATE, and DELETE commands where authorized to do so, and create views and synonyms.

Only the SYSADM can use this form of the GRANT command, and the authority to use it cannot be transferred to anyone else. The password that's associated with the creation of a new user is stored in a database area called the System Catalog. Both the SYSADM and the DBA can see passwords in the System Catalog, but only the SYSADM can change somebody else's password.

TIP

Individual users can change their own passwords at any time with the ALTER PASSWORD command. They cannot, however, change or even see anyone else's password.

Upgrading Authority Levels

Once a new user is established via the GRANT CONNECT command, the SYSADM can increase the user's authorization level by using the GRANT command with two different modifiers. First, the user can be granted RESOURCE-level authority. The SYSADM would type:

GRANT RESOURCE TO [user-name];

Once the SYSDAM gives users RESOURCE authority, they can create and drop tables and grant, change, or revoke privileges on those tables.

TIP

The authority to create and drop tables, and to grant, change, and revoke table privileges is added on top of all of the CONNECT-level authority.

Finally, the SYSADM can use the GRANT command to create new DBAs by typing:

GRANT DBA TO [user-name];

This level of authority gives users all CONNECT and RESOURCE privileges as well as all privileges on all tables in the database, plus the right to grant, change, or revoke other users' table privileges anywhere in the database.

TIP

The DBA cannot change the authority level of other users, nor change their passwords. These privileges, along with the ability to create new users, belong only to the SYSADM.

CHECK YOURSELF

1. Create a new user.

2. Increase the new user's authority to RESOURCE level.

3. Give the new user DBA authority.

ANSWERS

If you are the SQL superuser (SYSADM or some similar identity, depending on the DBMS program you are using), you perform all of the tasks associated with creating new users, assigning them passwords, and revising their authority levels through the GRANT command.

1. Type:
   GRANT CONNECT TO [user-name] IDENTIFIED BY [password];

2. Type:
   GRANT RESOURCE TO [user-name];

3. Type:
   GRANT DBA TO [user-name];

Privilege Levels

Privilege levels are different from authority levels. A user with CONNECT authority still has to receive specific permission to access individual tables. Users with RESOURCE authority still have to receive specific permission to access any table that anyone else creates.

Privilege levels are assigned by another use of the GRANT command. In this case, however, a different set of modifiers is used and both the DBA and RESOURCE-level users can invoke this kind of GRANT.

The modifiers used with this form of the GRANT command are: ALL, SELECT, INSERT, DELETE, INDEX, ALTER, and UPDATE.

If you are a SYSADM, DBA, or user with RESOURCE authority, you can GRANT privileges by typing:

GRANT ALL ON [table-name or view-name] TO [user-name] or [PUBLIC];

if you want to give someone the right to SELECT, INSERT, DELETE, UPDATE, INDEX, or ALTER information in a table or a view.

TIP

A SYSADM or a DBA can grant these privileges for any table or view in the database. A user with RESOURCE authority can only grant these privileges on tables or views he or she has personally created. Users with CONNECT authority cannot grant privileges and have none of their own unless those privileges are specifically granted by someone else.

The various privilege levels (with the exception of ALL) give users some relatively narrowly defined capabilities.

SELECT—Query a table or view.

INSERT—Add rows to a table or view.

DELETE—Remove rows from a table or view.

UPDATE—Update either a whole table or view or just specified columns in a particular table or view.

INDEX—Create or drop indexes for a table.

ALTER—Use the ALTER command to add, drop, rename, or modify a column.

TIP

If you wish to create an open table or view, you can use any of the above privilege levels, including the ALL privilege level, with the keyword PUBLIC in place of the [user-name] identifier. However, the PUBLIC keyword means that all future users, as well as all current users, will have the specified privilege level.

CHECK YOURSELF

1. Grant a user the ability to query a table.

2. Grant a user the ability to insert rows into a table.

3. Grant a user all privileges on a table.

4. Grant all database users all privileges on a table.

ANSWERS

1. Type:
   GRANT SELECT ON [table-name] TO [user-name];

2. Type:
   GRANT INSERT ON [table-name] TO [user-name];

3. Type:
   GRANT ALL ON [table-name] TO [user-name];

4. Type:
   GRANT ALL ON [table-name] TO PUBLIC;

REVOKE

The opposite of GRANT is REVOKE. Just as there are GRANT commands that bestow both authority levels and privilege levels, there are equal and opposite REVOKE commands that take away these same authority and privilege levels. Only the SYSADM can REVOKE authority levels by typing the command:

REVOKE [CONNECT, RESOURCE, or DBA] FROM [user-name];

You'll notice that the only difference between REVOKE and GRANT is that the REVOKE command does not require the SYS-ADM to enter the user's password.

REVOKE is a progressive command in the same way that GRANT is progressive. REVOKE DBA takes away a user's right to create or drop tables and to grant or revoke privileges for other users. The user retains CONNECT authority and any tables or views created by the user remain part of the database.

REVOKE RESOURCE likewise takes away the user's right to create or drop tables but not the user's CONNECT privileges. Again, any tables or views created by the user remain part of the database.

REVOKE CONNECT takes away the user's right to access the database. Before you can revoke a person's CONNECT privileges, however, you have to make sure they no longer own any tables. As long as a user owns a table, you can't REVOKE his or her CONNECT privileges.

TIP

The SYSADM authority level is irrevocable.

CHECK YOURSELF

1. Revoke a user's authority to create or drop tables and to grant or revoke privileges for other users.

2. Revoke a user's authority to create or drop tables.

3. Revoke a user's authority to access a database.

ANSWERS

1. Type:
   REVOKE DBA FROM [user-name];

2. Type:
   REVOKE RESOURCE FROM [user-name];

3. Type:
   REVOKE CONNECT FROM [user-name];

Revoking Privileges

Issuing a REVOKE command in relation to a user's privilege level follows the same pattern as issuing a GRANT command, only in reverse. Any user with a GRANT authority for a specific table or view can also issue a REVOKE command for that same table or view. A SYSADM or DBA has REVOKE authority for all tables and views in the database. A user with RESOURCE authority can issue REVOKE commands for the tables he or she personally creates. A user with CONNECT authority cannot issue REVOKE commands.

Issuing the command:

REVOKE ALL ON [table-name] PUBLIC;

would effectively close the table to everyone except the person who created that table and the SYSADM and/or the DBA.

ALTER PASSWORD

There are two ways a password can be changed in an SQL database. Either the SYSADM can change a user's password with the GRANT CONNECT command or the users can change their own passwords with the ALTER PASSWORD command.

If you are the SYSADM, typing:

GRANT CONNECT [user-name] IDENTIFIED BY [new password];

will lock a user out of the system. Only you or the DBA can see the user's password and the user cannot log onto the system without it.

If you are a user with DBA, RESOURCE, or CONNECT authority, you can change your own password by typing:

ALTER PASSWORD [old password] TO [new password];

TIP

Change your initial password as soon as you log on to a database for the first time. Default passwords are intentionally easy to guess, usually something like PASSWORD, for example, and those assigned by the SYSADM are generally simple, such as a repetition of your logon ID.

CHECK YOURSELF

1. Change your own password from COMMON to UNIQUE.

2. As SYSADM, change a user's password from OLD to NEW.

ANSWERS

1. Type:
   ALTER PASSWORD COMMON TO UNIQUE;

2. If you are the SYSADM you can type:
   GRANT CONNECT TO [user-name] IDENTIFIED BY NEW;

QUICK SUMMARY

In this chapter you've learned the reasons why you need database security and how to go about ensuring it as a system administrator and as a database administrator. Here are some of the important points in this chapter. The word or phrase in bold lists a relational database feature. That feature's definition and its benefit to you follows.

SYSADM The database superuser. Known by various labels, this user is the only one who can add new users, change somebody else's password, or change an existing authority level.

DBA The second most powerful persona in the SQL hierarchy. A DBA can view other user's passwords, has all privileges on all tables in the database, and can grant, change, or revoke anyone's table privileges.

RESOURCE One of two ordinary user authority levels. RESOURCE-level users can create and drop tables and grant, change, or revoke access privileges on the tables they create.

CONNECT The lowest authority level. CONNECT-level users cannot create or drop tables and can only access tables to which they have been given specific permission to access.

GRANT The command that creates new users and subsequently assigns them their authority levels. Also, the command that assigns the ability to query or modify any table or view.

REVOKE The opposite of GRANT, REVOKE takes away a user's authority and/or privilege levels.

ALTER PASSWORD The command a user invokes to change his or her own password.

PRACTICE WHAT YOU'VE LEARNED

1. What are the four levels of SQL users?

2. What are the authority levels for each?

3. Create a new user.

4. Increase the new user's authority to RESOURCE level.

5. Give the new user DBA authority.

6. Grant a user the ability to query a table.

7. Grant a user the ability to insert rows into a table.

8. Grant a user all privileges on a table.

9. Grant all database users all privileges on a table.

10. Revoke a user's authority to create or drop tables and to grant or revoke privileges for other users.

11. Revoke a user's authority to create or drop tables.

12. Revoke a user's authority to access a database.

13. Change your own password from COMMON to UNIQUE.

14. As SYSADM, change a user's password from OLD to NEW.

ANSWERS

1. System administrator (SYSADM), database administrator (DBA), users with the authority to create new tables (RESOURCE), and users with access authority only (CONNECT).

2. The SYSADM has the highest level authority and can create new users, assign authority levels, and change passwords; the DBA has all privileges on all tables and can assign or modify privileges for other users; the RESOURCE user can create and drop tables and can assign privileges for other users in those tables; the CONNECT user has access authority, but only when specifically granted.

3. Type:
   GRANT CONNECT TO [user-name] IDENTIFIED BY [password];

4. Type:
   GRANT RESOURCE TO [user-name];

5. Type:
   GRANT DBA TO [user-name];

6. Type:
   GRANT SELECT ON [table-name] TO [user-name];

7. Type:
   GRANT INSERT ON [table-name] TO [user-name];

8. Type:
   GRANT ALL ON [table-name] TO [user-name];

9. Type:
   GRANT ALL ON [table-name] TO PUBLIC;

10. Type:
    REVOKE DBA FROM [user-name];

11. Type:
    REVOKE RESOURCE FROM [user-name];

12. Type:
    REVOKE CONNECT FROM [user-name];

13. Type:
    ALTER PASSWORD COMMON TO UNIQUE;

14. If you are the SYSADM you can type:
    GRANT CONNECT TO [user-name] IDENTIFIED BY NEW;

Embedded SQL

Embedded SQL refers to the process of including SQL commands in programs written in a procedural language, such as C. In this chapter, you will learn about:

▲ **Using SQL as part of a procedural language**

▲ **Managing program flow**

▲ **Managing data flow**

▲ **Using cursors to locate data**

▲ **Transaction processing**

Using SQL as Part of a Procedural Language

As we noted earlier, SQL is not a programming language in that it does not provide procedural logic, extensive data typing, or variables. SQL confines itself to manipulating database objects.

If you want to write an application program (in C for example) that will access a database, you embed SQL commands within the C program. SQL is then used within the application program to perform the strictly database functions.

In order for the procedural language and SQL to interact, they need a host language interface to act as a translator between the procedural language and the database language. Such translators are termed, "applications programming interfaces," or "APIs." When you use an API, any SQL statements embedded within the procedural-language code are processed together with the source code through an external precompiler. The precompiler calls the API to parse and compile the SQL statements. The API replaces the SQL statements with appropriate source code calls and hands everything back to the run-time DBMS interface. You wind up with a modified source program, which then goes through the normal process of compiling and linking and results in an executable program. This is known as a precompiler-type API.

An alternative method of embedding SQL statements in a procedural language involves the use of a language-specific library of function calls. What you do here is embed the function calls in the source code. After you compile the program you link it with the API library. You compile the source program in the normal way for that language, with linking to the API library taking place during the normal link phase. This is known as a library-type API.

Most library-type APIs will have function calls that let your application establish a connection with the database program, compile a statement, execute the statement, retrieve result rows, and break the connection to the database. Beyond that, you'll generally also have functions that return status information.

The library approach avoids the precompilation step that is part of the precompiler, or nonlibrary, approach. It also provides more specific functions for operating in the database, such as the ability to run in result-set mode, the ability to connect to multiple databases and the ability to perform on-line backups and restores. Usually, constructs such as cursors are also automatically supported when you use a library-type API.

On the other hand, APIs that use libraries tend to be more closely identified with a particular DBMS package, making the code less portable. The precompiler approach has the advantage of being easier to move from one platform to another and one DBMS to another, as long as the appropriate precompiler is available for that platform.

The end result is pretty much the same, whichever method you use. The precompiler approach has the benefit of greater portability while the library approach is simpler.

Using SQL as Part of a Procedural Language

CHECK YOURSELF

What are the two different ways you can embed SQL statements in a procedural language?

ANSWER

The two approaches are the precompiler method and the library method. The precompiler method takes care of generating source code from your SQL statements and is more portable. The library approach requires that you enter the source code but avoids the need for a separate precompiler. The library approach also incorporates constructs for database access and cursor support, which have to be created separately if you use the precompiler method.

Managing Program Flow

Program flow refers to the internals of the procedural language. Program flow is that part of the programming language that tells the computer to perform certain actions in a particular sequence.

Languages like C and COBOL are programming (or procedural) languages and, as such, are designed for the express purpose of telling a computer what to do and when to do it. SQL is not a programming language. However, because SQL statements can be embedded in procedural languages, you can write a program in C, for example, add SQL statements when you want your program to manipulate data in a database, and revert back to C when the data manipulation is done. In the example listing below, from the Gupta Technologies *C/API Reference Manual* for SQLBase, a C program designed to show how to use C/API functions in Microsoft Windows illustrates the intermixing of standard C language functions with specific SQLBase functions. The C language guides the execution of the program as a whole, while the embedded SQL commands deal with the interaction of the program with SQLBase and with the manipulation of data in a database.

```
/* COPYRIGHT (C) GUPTA TECHNOLOGIES, INC. 1984-1990 */
/*
 Copyright (c) 1989 Gupta Technologies, Inc.
 All Rights Reserved.
/*

Function Name:
  TestSQLSample

Parameters:
  HWND              Handle of the main window

Returns:
  BOOL              TRUE for success, FALSE for
failure.

Description:
  This procedure performs the following steps
(command line options can be used to skip steps
or modify the behavior of steps):

    The database is connected to by calling
sqlcon and passing the database name string.
```

The table is created by calling *sqlcex*
with the CREATE TABLE string.

TestSQLInsert is called to insert fields
read from a file into the table.

The index is created by calling *sqlcex*
with the CREATE INDEX string.

TestSQLSelect is called to select the
fields inserted into the table.

The database is disconnected from by
calling *sqldis*.

Dynamic library resources are freed by
calling *sqldon*.
*/

```
BOOL      TestSQLSample(hWnd)
HWND                  hWnd;
{
int               nRuns;              /* number of
runs               */
FARPROC   lpProcInst;
char       cMsgBuffer[200];
BOOL     bStatus;            /* return code
*/

bStatus = FALSE;
lpProcInst = NULL;

/* initialize cursor number    */;
gCursor = 0;

  /* initialize dynamic API library */
  if (gRetCode =
```

```
        sqlini(lpProcInst =
MakeProcInstance(TestYieldProc, hInst)))
  {
    TestLogMessage("Cannot initialize API
interface - %u\n", gRetCode);
    Goto errexit;
  }
  else
    bgSQLInit = TRUE;

  TestLogMessage("Connecting to database\n");

  /* set number of pages */
  sqlscp(15);

  /* connect To the database */
  if (gRetCode = sqlcnc(&gCursor, szgDBName, 0))
  {
    TestLogSQLFailure("CONNECT");
    TestLogMessage(TESTINITMSG);
    MessageBox(hWnd, TESTCOPYMSG,
TESTWINDOWCAPTION, MB_OK | MB_ICONHAND);
    Goto errexit;
  }

  /* not doing query only?              */
  if (!bgQueryOnly)
  {
    TestLogMessage("%s\n", szgCreateTableCmd);

    /* Compile and execute create table */
    if (sqlcex(gCursor, szgCreateTableCmd, 0))
  {
      TestLogSQLFailure("CREATE TABLE");
      TestLogMessage(TESTINITMSG);
      MessageBox(hWnd, TESTCOPYMSG,
TESTWINDOWCAPTION, MB_OK | MB_ICONHAND);
      Goto errexit;
    }
```

```
  /* Insert records from input file */
  if (!TestSQLInsert())
    Goto errexit;


  TestLogMessage("%s\n", szgCreateIndexCmd);

  /* create the index */
  if (sqlcex(gCursor, szgCreateIndexCmd, 0))
{
    TestLogSQLFailure("CREATE INDEX");
    Goto errexit;
  }

  TestLogMessage("COMMIT\n");

  /* commit the changes */
  if (sqlcmt(gCursor))
  {
    TestLogSQLFailure("COMMIT");
    Goto errexit;
  }
}  /* end of if (!bgQueryOnly) */

/* select fields from table */
for (nRuns = 0; nRuns < gNumRuns; nRuns++)
  if (!TestSQLSelect())
    Goto errexit;


TestLogMessage("Disconnect from database\n");
/* disconnect  from the database */
if (gRetCode = sqldis(gCursor))
{
  /* indicate invalid cursor            */
  gCursor = 0;
  TestLogSQLFailure("DISCONNECT");
```

```
        Goto errexit;
    }

    bStatus = TRUE;

errexit:

    if (bgSQLInit)
        {
        /* free resources allocated to dynamic API
library                                   */
        sqldon();
        bgSQLInit = FALSE;
        }

    if (lpProcInst)
        FreeProcInstance(lpProcInst);

    sprintf(cMsgBuffer, "Output has also been
printed to file \"%s\"\n",
                szgLogFileName);
    TestLogMessage(cMsgBuffer);
    TestLogMessage("*****\n");

    return bStatus;
}


/*
```

The foregoing segments of the Gupta Technologies, Inc., program *ex21.c* show the way the procedural language and the query language work together to create, index, query, and disconnect from a table, all through embedded SQL.

CHECK YOURSELF

What is program flow?

ANSWER

Program flow is the order in which a procedural language program, such as an application written in C, handles the execution of commands.

Managing Data Flow

While program flow, as explained above, manages the order in which an application program generally performs its task, data flow manages the order in which the specific SQL procedures are carried out. The following flow chart from the SQLBase *C/API Reference Manual* shows the sequence of operations that perform a SELECT command.

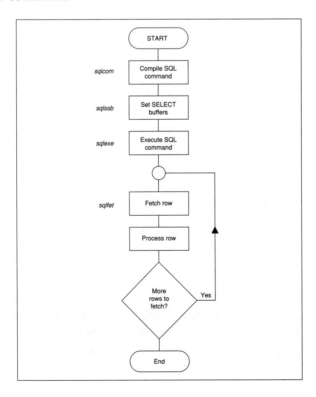

Some of the points that the flow chart illustrates include: an SQL command must be compiled before it can be executed; the *sqlssb* function sets up the data area in the program where the data for each column fetched by *sqlfet* is received; the *sqlexe* function executes the previously compiled command; after a SELECT command is executed, the *sqlfet* function retrieves one row at a time until all rows in the result set are fetched.

CHECK YOURSELF

What is data flow?

ANSWER

Data flow is a set of procedures, specific to SQL, that rest inside the more general procedures defined by the program flow.

Using Cursors to Locate Data

One of the characteristics of SQL is that it is a set-oriented language. On top of that, most applications require row-by-row (or record-by-record) data access. Because of the way the language's set orientation interacts with the application's data access requirements, the position of data becomes very important. Keeping track of data positions is easier when you have a marker.

You can set the marker at a particular spot (the current row position in a result table) and tell the program that you want, for example, the next row of information, or the previous row of information, or a row of information ten rows below the position of the marker. The SQL name for these markers is "cursor."

SQL also uses the word "cursor" to mean "a work space in memory used for processing an SQL command" and "a handle that identifies a database connection." It may not seem so, but all of these meanings are really different ways of talking about the same thing.

The reason cursors are included as part of our discussion of embedded SQL is that cursors are extra constructs that you must supply when using embedded SQL. Without creating, or DECLARING, a cursor you can't use embedded SQL to access your database from the procedural language. What that means is that, when your application connects to a database, the cursor handle is returned and you use that cursor handle in further embedded SQL functions to identify your connection.

Using Cursors to Locate Data

CHECK YOURSELF

1. What is a cursor?

2. Why is it important?

ANSWERS

1. A cursor is a construct in embedded SQL that defines the current row position in a result table.

2. The cursor becomes the location marker from which subsequent operations are carried out.

DECLARE Cursor

The first step in using a cursor is to DECLARE it. This command has various names, depending on the SQL DBMS you're using. In SQLBase, for example, it's called CONNECT. Generally, you only use this declaration command when you want to change the existing cursor or when you want to create more than one cursor in a given database. That's because, in most SQL DBMS programs, a primary cursor is automatically generated when you connect to the database.

To declare a cursor in SQLBase, you would type, for example:

CONNECT [database-name] [cursor-number];

at the main DBMS prompt. This would have the effect of creating a second cursor (i.e., "connection") to the database specified with the [database-name] parameter.

TIP

No matter how many connections you establish, only one database and one cursor is active or "current" at any given time. The active cursor is the one you *most recently* created.

If you just want to create a new cursor to the current database, you can leave out the [database-name] parameter altogether. The DBMS will default to the current database in the absence of a [database-name].

CHECK YOURSELF

1. Declare a new cursor in the current database.

2. Declare a new cursor to use for accessing a second database.

ANSWERS

1. At the DBMS prompt, type:
   CONNECT 2;

2. At the DBMS prompt, type:
   CONNECT [database-name] 2;

SET CURSORNAME

The SET CURSORNAME command is used in situations where you are working with more than one cursor in a database. You would type the command:

SET CURSORNAME [cursor-name];

at the database prompt before executing an UPDATE or DELETE with a CURRENT OF clause or as part of an INSERT command with an ADJUSTING clause. Such a command statement assigns a name to the current cursor and lets you INSERT data into a result set without invalidating the result set. The rows you INSERT are added to the end of the result set and to the database.

USE

The USE command activates one or another of the cursors you have created or DECLARED. You use it to switch between the cursors in a multicursor operation after a CONNECT has been used to create the cursors. For example, if you establish a connection to a database for another user and then want to work in that database yourself, you could switch between the cursors (or active connections) by typing:

USE 1;
when you want to assume control of the connection and:

USE 2;
when you want the other user to access the database.

Alternatively, if you are working in more than one database at a time, you would employ the USE command and give yourself a different cursor number in each of the databases. In database 1 you would have cursor 1, while in database 2 you could have cursor 2 or a cursor name you created with the SET CURSORNAME command. Thereafter, whenever you wanted to switch between databases you would type the USE command followed by the cursor name or number that relates to the target database.

CHECK YOURSELF

Switch your active connection from database 1 to database 2, where you have used the default connection for database 1 and given the second database connection the name cursor 2.

ANSWER

At the DBMS prompt, type:
USE 2;

FETCH

Once you have set up the connections that let you perform a variety of actions by embedding them in your procedural language program, you can FETCH data that you want to manipulate. You use FETCH as part of a SELECT procedure to limit the number of rows you need to work with at any given time. For example, if you unembedded the SELECT command in your application, you would get a result set composed of all the rows that matched your selection criteria. You would then use the FETCH command to call up the first row for processing. Subsequent FETCHes would call succeeding rows, in order, until all of the rows are processed. The following program from the *SQLBase C/API Reference Manual* illustrates how you would use the FETCH command in a C program to fetch rows from a result set.

Copyright (c) 1989 Gupta Technologies, Inc.
 All Rights Reserved.

```
#include "sql.h"


/*------------------------------------------------
-----------------*/
/*
*/
/*   Example of a simple fetch
*/
/*
*/
/*   Run EMP.SQL via SQLTALK to initialize
tables and data       */
/*
*/
/*------------------------------------------------
-----------------*/

          SQLTCUR    cur;
/* SQLBASE cursor number   */
```

```
                SQLTRCD    rcd;
/* error number              */
             char          errmsg[SQLMERR];
/* error msg text buffer  */

             main()
{
               char                  name[20];
/* employe name buffer          */

static    char       selcmd [] =              /*
SQL SELECT statement    */
"SELECT EMP_NAME FROM EMP ORDER BY EMP_NAME";

  /*
    CONNECT TO THE DATABASE
  */

  if (rcd = sqlcnc(&cur, "DEMO", 0))
  {
    sqlerr(rcd, errmsg);
/* get error message text */
    printf("%s \n",errmsg);
    exit(1);
  }

  /*
    COMPILE SELECT STATEMENT
  */

  if (sqlcom(cur, selcmd, 0))
    failure("SELECT COMPILE");

  /*
    SET UP SELECT BUFFER
  */

  if (sqlssb(cur, 1, SQLPBUF, name, 20, 0,
SQLNPTR, SQLNPTR))
```

```
          failure("SET SELECT BUFFER");

     /*
       EXECUTE SELECT STATEMENT
     */

     if (sqlexe(cur))
       failure("EXECUTING SELECT");

     /*
       FETCH DATA
     */

     for (;;)
     {
       memset(name,' ',20);                              /*
clear employe name buf */

       if (rcd = sqlfet(cur))
/* fetch the data         */
          break;

       printf("%s \n", name);
/* print employe name           */
     }

    if (rcd != 1)
/* failure on fetch               */
       failure("FETCH");

      /*
        DISCONNECT FROM THE DATABASE
      */

     if (rcd = sqldis(cur))
       failure("DISCONNECT");
}

              failure(ep)
```

```
            char*      ep;
/* -> failure msg string  */
{
            SQLTEPO    epo;                  /*
error position                 */

  printf("Failure on %s \n", ep);
  sqlrcd(cur, &rcd);
/* get the error              */
  sqlepo(cur, &epo);
/* get error position         */
  sqlerr(rcd, errmsg);
/* get error message text */
  sqldis(cur);
  printf("%s (error: %u, position: %u)
\n",errmsg,rcd,epo);
  exit(1);
}
```

CHECK YOURSELF

What does a FETCH command do?

ANSWER

A FETCH command in embedded SQL retrieves rows from a result table. It retrieves the rows one at a time for processing.

OPEN

In the example program above there is a specific command (*sqlcnc*) that the application uses to establish the connection to the database, or OPEN it. This has to be a part of any procedural language process if you want to perform operations on a database. The short example below illustrates the principle in isolation:

```
#include "sql.h"

/*--------------------------------------------------
-----------------*/
/*
*/
/*  Example of simple connect using all
standard defaults           */
/*
*/
/*--------------------------------------------------
-----------------*/

                main()
{
                SQLTCUR    cur;
/* SQLBASE cursor number   */
                SQLTRCD    rcd;
/* return code                              */

  /*
     CONNECT TO THE DATABASE
  */

  if (rcd = sqlcnc(&cur, "DEMO", 0))
  {
    printf("FAILURE ON CONNECT %d\n",rcd);
    exit(1);
  }
  else
    printf("Connection Established \n");
```

CLOSE

Likewise, when you leave the database after performing your specific data manipulations, CLOSE the connection to the database. In the example below, the CLOSE, or DISCONNECT, function is handled by the function call, *sqldis*:

Copyright (c) 1989 Gupta Technologies, Inc.
All Rights Reserved.

```
/*

    DISCONNECT FROM THE DATABASE
  */

  if (rcd = sqldis(cur))
    printf("FAILURE ON DISCONNECT %d\n",rcd);
  else
    printf("Disconnect Performed \n");
}
```

CHECK YOURSELF

What commands do you need to embed in your procedural language program to OPEN and CLOSE a database connection?

ANSWER

The specific function calls may vary slightly, depending on the individual DBMS program, but they will accomplish the task of connecting to and disconnecting from the database. In SQLBase's C language API, these functions are represented by the *sqlcnc* and *sqldis* function calls.

Transaction Processing

Once you have established your connection to the database and defined your cursor, you need an efficient way of manipulating data in the database's table and views. The concept of a "transaction" was devised to provide this kind of efficiency.

A transaction is a logical unit of work that treats several SQL commands as a unit. The program controls when a transaction done by a program is made permanent or erased from the database.

A logical unit of work is a sequence of SQL commands treated as a single entity. All the SQL commands are made permanent at the same time, or they are undone together. For example, a logical unit of work might add money to one account and remove it from another account. Both operations would be done with an UPDATE command. If both UPDATES are treated in the same unit of work, then the database is not in danger of being left in an inconsistent state; either both UPDATES are made permanent or neither one is.

In embedded SQL the *sqlcmt* function performs the same role as an SQL COMMIT command and the *sqlrbk* function performs the same job as an SQL ROLLBACK command. The COMMIT process makes a change permanent. The ROLLBACK process erases a transaction from the database. The COMMIT and ROLLBACK commands are standard SQL commands and are common to all varieties of SQL databases.

COMMIT and ROLLBACK

COMMIT and ROLLBACK keep your data safe. With the COMMIT command, all of your changes are made at once so you don't wind up with partially updated data. ROLLBACK removes or erases any changes made since the last COMMIT command and restores the database to its most recent saved condition.

SAVEPOINT

A failure during a large data input or update process doesn't necessarily mean that you must go back and do everything over again from the point where the last COMMIT was made. The concept of a SAVEPOINT takes care of preserving some of your data. A SAVEPOINT (sometimes called a CHECKPOINT, depending on the DBMS) is an intermediate point within a transaction. You can set these CHECKPOINTS or SAVEPOINTS when you format your ROLLBACK statement. By setting a SAVEPOINT you provide yourself with the safety of making, in effect, subsidiary COMMIT commands. You save everything up to that point. A later ROLL-BACK or a system failure will mean that you only undo your changes or lose your data back as far as the last SAVEPOINT.

The SAVEPOINT is specified as an option in the ROLLBACK command. In the sample code below, you can see how to set up a transaction processing procedure that includes COMMIT and ROLLBACK:

Copyright (c) 1989 Gupta Technologies, Inc.
All Rights Reserved.

```
#include "sql.h"

/*-------------------------------------------------
-----------------*/
/*
*/
/*  Classic example of transferring money from
saving account to  */
/*  checking account employing a ROLLBACK if
either update fails  */
/*  and a COMMIT of the transaction if both
update succeed      */
/*
*/
/*-------------------------------------------------
-----------------*/
```

```
                main()
{
                SQLTCUR    cur;                    /*
SQLBASE cursor number    */
                SQLTRCD    rcd;                    /*
return code                              */

static    char       savupdt [] =          /*
UPDATE savings command */
"UPDATE SAVINGS SET SAV_DOLLARS = SAV_DOLLARS -
100 WHERE SAV_ACC_NO = 951";

static    char       chkupdt [] =          /*
UPDATE checking command*/
"UPDATE CHECKING SET CHK_DOLLARS = CHK_DOLLARS
+ 100 WHERE CHK_ACC_NO = 1495";

  /*
    CONNECT TO THE DATABASE
  */

  if (rcd = sqlcnc(&cur, "DEMO", 0))
  {
    printf("FAILURE ON CONNECT %d\n",rcd);
    exit(1);
  }
  else
    printf("Connection Established \n");

  /*
    COMPILE AND EXECUTE UPDATE OF SAVINGS
ACCOUNT
  */

  if (rcd = sqlcex(cur, savupdt, 0))
  {
    printf("FAILED UPDATING SAVINGS, rcd =
%d\n",rcd);
```

```
      sqldis(cur);
      exit(1);
   }
   else
      printf("ONE HUNDRED DOLLARS SUBTRACTED FROM
SAVINGS \n");

   /*
      COMPILE AND EXECUTE UPDATE OF CHECKING
ACCOUNT
   */

   if (rcd = sqlcex(cur, chkupdt, 0))
   {
      printf("FAILED UPDATING CHECKING
(TRANSACTION ROLLBACK), rcd = %d\n",rcd);
      sqlrbk(cur);
      sqldis(cur);
      exit(1);
   }
   else
      printf("ONE HUNDRED DOLLARS ADDED TO
CHECKING \n");

   /*
      COMMIT TRANSACTION
   */

   if (rcd = sqlcmt(cur))
      printf("FAILURE ON COMMIT, rcd = %d\n",rcd);
   else
      printf("TRANSFER FROM SAVINGS TO CHECKING
COMPLETED \n");

   /*
      DISCONNECT FROM THE DATABASE
   */

   if (rcd = sqldis(cur))
```

```
        printf("FAILURE ON DISCONNECT %d\n",rcd);
    else
        printf("Disconnect Performed \n");
}
```

CHECK YOURSELF

1. What is the purpose of the COMMIT and ROLLBACK functions?

2. What is a SAVEPOINT?

ANSWERS

1. COMMIT processes your entire transaction at one time. It prevents situations in which only part of a transaction might be saved, thus preventing imbalances in the database. ROLLBACK provides for the erasure of all data back to the point of the last COMMIT command. In this way, if you have a system failure during a transaction, you don't wind up with partially saved or incomplete records.

2. A SAVEPOINT is an intermediate position inside a transaction. You use SAVEPOINTs as markers. You can ROLLBACK to a SAVEPOINT to cancel any subsequent commands and you can execute a COMMIT at a SAVEPOINT to save your work up to that point.

QUICK SUMMARY

In this chapter we've learned the basics of embedded SQL. Here are some of the important points in this chapter. The word or phrase in bold lists a relational database feature. That feature's definition and its benefit to you follows.

Program flow Program flow is the process of controlling the actions of a procedural language application's commands when that application includes SQL statements.

Data flow   Data flow is the process of controlling the manipulation of database objects when they are operated on by SQL commands embedded inside a procedural language program.

Cursors   A cursor is the position of a row with a *result table*. The word cursor is also used to mean a work space in memory and, finally, it refers to an individual connection to a database.

FETCH   A FETCH is the process of retrieving rows from a database.

OPEN   OPEN is a generic SQL term that means to establish a connection to a database. In some implementations of SQL it is referred to by the word CONNECT.

CLOSE   CLOSE is a generic SQL term that means to disconnect from a database. In some implementations of SQL it is referred to by the word DISCONNECT.

COMMIT   To COMMIT a transaction means to save it. When you execute a COMMIT, you save the entire transaction, all at once.

ROLLBACK   To ROLLBACK a transaction means to erase it. When you execute a ROLLBACK, you erase the entire transaction, back to the point where it was last COMMITTED, or saved.

SAVEPOINT   A SAVEPOINT is an intermediate position within a transaction. You can COMMIT at a SAVEPOINT to save your work up to that point. Later, you can ROLLBACK to the last SAVEPOINT to cancel your most recent actions.

PRACTICE WHAT YOU'VE LEARNED

1.   What are the two different ways you can embed SQL statements in a procedural language?

2.   What is program flow?

3.   What is data flow?

4.   What is a cursor?

5.   Why is cursor important?

6.   Declare a new cursor in the current database.

7. Declare a new cursor to use for accessing a second database.

8. Switch your active connection from database 1 to database 2, where you have used the default connection for database 1 and given the second database connection the name cursor 2.

9. What does a FETCH command do?

10. What commands do you need to embed in your procedural language program to OPEN and CLOSE a database connection?

ANSWERS

1. The two approaches are the precompiler method and the library method. The precompiler method takes care of generating source code from your SQL statements and is more portable. The library approach requires that you enter the source code but avoids the need for a separate precompiler. The library approach also incorporates constructs for database access and cursor support, which have to be created separately if you use the precompiler method.

2. Program flow is the order in which a procedural language program, such as an application written in C, handles the execution of commands.

3. Data flow is a set of procedures, specific to SQL, that rest inside the more general procedures defined by the program flow.

4. A cursor is a construct in embedded SQL that defines the current row position in a result table.

5. The cursor becomes the location marker from which subsequent operations are carried out.

6. At the DBMS prompt, type:
   CONNECT 2;

7. At the DBMS prompt, type:
   CONNECT [database-name] 2;

8. At the DBMS prompt, type:
   USE 2;

9. A FETCH command in embedded SQL retrieves rows from a result table. It retrieves the rows one at a time for processing.

10. The specific function calls may vary slighlty, depending on the individual DBMS program, but they will accomplish the task of connecting to and disconnecting from the database. In SQLBase's C language API, these functions are represented by the *sqlcnc* and *sqldis* function calls.

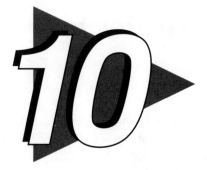

Other SQL Systems

While there is a core structured query language composed of standard statements and procedures as defined by the American National Standards Institute, the core statements serve as the skeleton on which commercial products like SQLBase are built. Each DBMS producer has a particular idea of what constitutes the best way to use SQL for the task of handling data. As a result different SQL implementations are built around added statements, called *extensions*, that give you extra capabilities. In this chapter we'll take a look at:

▲ How SQLBase relates to other DBMS

▲ SQLBase extensions

▲ Functions

▲ Other file server database systems

▲ Client-Server database management systems

How SQLBase Relates to Other DBMSs

SQLBase and SQLTalk represent Gupta Technologies' particular vision of SQL. As you know, SQLBase is Gupta's DBMS. SQLTalk (in either character mode or Windows mode) is the language *interface* that mediates between you and the program. In this respect, SQLBase has similarities with other highly developed DBMS. Products such as SQL Server from Sybase, Inc. (and its PC version as introduced by Microsoft) have its version of SQL, called Transact-SQL.

On the one hand, you have the DBMS, on the other, you have the particular version of SQL that communicates with the DBMS, along with its individualized user interface. Both SQLTalk and Transact-SQL are examples of client software. You use them on your individual PC and they form your primary means of communicating with your data. Full implementations of DBMS also usually include a programming interface, such as Gupta's C/API and COBOL SQL Precompiler, or SQL Server's DB-LIBRARY.

Each of these combinations of products (DBMS, language interface, applications programming interface) should be looked at as an aggregate, with all of the individual pieces contributing to the final product that, for convenience, generally goes by the name of the DBMS component. As a result, when people talk about SQLBase, they generally have in mind the DBMS (SQLBase), the language (SQLTalk/Character and/or SQLTalk/Windows) and the programming interface (the precompiler and/or API). A similar reference to SQL Server would be expanded to include Transact-SQL and its command-line utility called *isql* and/or its Windows interface, known as SAF (Server Adminstration Facility), and the programming interface DB-LIBRARY.

We don't want to go too far in drawing similarities between SQLBase and SQL Server. They are different products and have distinguishing characteristics that set them apart from each other. The point of the information above is simply to establish that full-blown DBMSs consist of several parts and, in many cases, those parts will bear certain similarities.

What distinguishes different DBMSs is often the emphasis each places on what it is built to do, how it goes about accessing and manipulating data, and whether it is more open or less open to other client software. In this regard, SQLBase prides itself on providing a relatively complete environment although data can be imported from, and exported to, other file formats. SQL Server's developers, on the other hand, emphasize its ability to interact with third-party client software. One school of thought emphasizes the efficiency and speed of a dedicated approach, while the other emphasizes the benefits of being open to a wide variety of software products.

Moreover, different SQL implementations are built to operate in different environments (standalone PCs, local area networks (LAN), on minicomputers, or on mainframes) and, as mentioned above, to be wholly (or largely) self-contained or to operate in close cooperation with programs. SQLBase is a DBMS that was designed to operate either on a standalone PC or in a LAN environment. Oracle, on the other hand, was developed for a minicomputer and mainframe environment but can use PCs as well as CRTs in its later versions. SQL Server is primarily a LAN-oriented product. dBase IV SQL and Paradox SQL were created from standalone PC products and have been given connectivity features that let them communicate with a database server.

How SQLBase Relates to Other DBMSs

CHECK YOURSELF

1. What are the main parts of an SQL system?

2. What distinguishes SQL systems?

ANSWERS

1. SQL systems are generally composed of the DBMS (or back-end), the SQL language interface (the front-end or client), and a programming interface for one or more procedural languages (either/or precompilers and applications programming interfaces).

2. Each vendor of SQL-based DBMS systems has given a particular emphasis to the environment, the development history, and the uses to which their products will be put. While most will work in a networked environment, for example, some were developed with mainframes in mind, while others were specifically created for a LAN environment, and still others were developed initially for standalone PCs and have been retrofit to operate over networks.

SQLBase Extensions

A prime characteristic that sets one product off from another in the SQL field is the way in which that product *extends* the ANSI Standard SQL. Extensions come in two varieties. They are either additions to standard SQL statements or they are entirely new SQL statements that the DBMS developer has added. SQLBase's language, SQLTalk, has SQL command extensions for session control, environment control, report writing, storing procedures and commands, and database administration. Here's a summary of SQLTalk's extensions to standard SQL and what actions the commands perform.

BACKUP Backs up a database or database logs, or both.

BREAK Specifies breaks for a report by inserting blank lines.

BTITLE Displays a report's title on the bottom of each page (a running foot line).

COLUMN Specifies column attributes for a report (heading, width, line wrap, etc.).

COMPUTE Computes aggregates for a report (SUM, AVG, MIN, MAX, COUNT).

CONNECT Connects the user to a database or cursor.

COPY Copies a database or table from a source table to an existing destination table in the same or a different database.

CREATE DATABASE Physically creates a database on the server specified by the SET SERVER command and installs it on the network.

DEINSTALL DATABASE Takes a database off the network and updates the *dbname* keyword in the SQL initialization file (*sql.ini*).

DELETE DATABASE Physically deletes the entire database directory for a database including all associated transaction log files on the server.

DISCONNECT Disconnects from a database or cursor. The last DISCONNECT for a database invokes the COMMIT command for that database.

EDIT Temporarily transfers control to the DOS line editor (EDLIN) or the UNIX line editor (vi) or a text editor you specify by setting the environment variable EDITOR.

ERASE Removes a stored SQL command.

EXECUTE Executes a stored SQL command.

EXIT Exits SQLTalk and returns you to your operating system prompt. It disconnects all cursors and causes a COMMIT to be executed for all cursors and databases.

FETCH Fetches rows from a result set and can only be used in result set mode or after you execute a PERFORM command.

INSTALL DATABASE Puts a database on the network.

LEFT Shifts displayed output of a SELECT command to begin with a column to the left of the current first column on your screen.

LIST Displays the most recently input command from the edit buffer.

LOAD Loads one or more tables from an external file into the current database.

PAUSE Suspends your current session until you press the <Enter> key and is used to cause a time lapse between groups of commands or to mark a transition point.

PERFORM Executes a PREPARE SQL command and must be invoked immediately after the PREPARE command.

How SQLBase Relates to Other DBMSs

PREPARE   Compiles but does not execute an SQL command. The command is parsed, syntax errors are checked, the existence of database objects is verified, a security check is performed, an optimal access path is determined, and the command is translated into executable modules.

PRINT   Prints a report to a printer or file and causes a specified command file to be run.

RELEASE LOG   Releases the current log file in preparation for backing it up and deleting it.

REMARK   Displays explanatory text on the output screen.

REORGANIZE   Reorganizes the database by unloading the database to a file, initializing the database, and reloading the database. The process unfragments database files.

RESTORE   Restores a backed up database or database log.

RIGHT   Displays the output of a SELECT command to the right of the first column on the screen.

ROLLFORWARD   Recovers a database by applying log files to bring a backup up to date after a RESTORE command has been issued.

RUN   Executes the commands stored in an SQLTalk command file.

SAVE   Writes the most recent SQL command or a series of SQLTalk commands to an executable file that can be RUN.

SET   Sets environment options for SQLTalk sessions.

SET SERVER   Establishes a connection to a server.

SET SPOOL   Records the SQLTalk session, records all screen activity in a file, but does not affect the screen display.

SHOW   Shows the value of a variable or attribute specified by the SET command.

SHOW DATABASES   Displays a list of available databases on a given server.

STORE   Compiles and stores a query or data manipulation command prior to executing that command or erasing it.

TITLE   Displays the running header of a report.

UNDO Used in restriction mode to revert to the previous result set (prior to the last SELECT command).

UNLOAD Unloads a database to an external file that can be in SQL format, ASCII format, or DIF format.

USE Selects a new current cursor and lets you switch between cursors in multicursor transactions.

$ Executes a native operating system (DOS, OS/2, UNIX) command by temporarily transferring control to the operating system. You are returned to SQLTalk when the operating system finishes executing the specified command.

How SQLBase Relates to Other DBMSs

CHECK YOURSELF

What are extensions and what purpose to they serve?

ANSWER

Extensions are commands added to the standard SQL language to increase, improve, or refine the language's ability to manipulate data, perform queries, and control data and transactions.

Functions

Because DBMS packages manipulate data to generate the information you request, they are built to perform classical computing activities, things like adding, subtracting, multiplying, and dividing. The way they use these strictly mathematical capabilities to present you with such an enormous variety of information in such a wide range of formats is through the exercise of special routines called *functions*. SQLBase's set of functions for handling text, dates and numbers falls into seven specialized classes: aggregate, string, date and time, logical, "special," math, and finance.

Aggregate functions compute a summary value from a group of values. They include:

AVG The average of the values you input.

COUNT The total of the items you specify.

MAX The maximum (or highest) value in the argument.

MIN The minimum (or smallest) value in the argument.

SUM Different from COUNT. Returns the sum of the values in the argument.

@SDV Computes the standard deviation for the set of values you specify.

String functions give you information about data represented as text. They include:

@CHAR Returns the ASCII character when you type in the character's decimal code.

@CODE The opposite of @CHAR, returns the decimal code for an ASCII character.

@EXACT This function compares two strings.

@FIND Returns the position inside one string of information contained in a second string.

@LEFT Returns a string (for a specified length) starting with the string's leftmost character.

@LENGTH Tells you the length of a string (number of characters).

@LOWER Converts uppercase letters to lowercase.

@MID Tells you the length of a string from a specified point to the end.

@NULLVALUE Written as @NULLVALUE(x,y), this function returns the string or number specified by y if x is null.

@PROPER Converts the first character of a string to uppercase and the rest to lowercase.

@REPEAT Creates a string of pattern repetitions by concatenating a string with itself for as many times as you specify.

@REPLACE Replaces characters in one string with the characters you specify from a second string.

@RIGHT Returns a specified number of characters in a right to left direction.

@SCAN This function searches a string for a pattern you declare and tells you where the pattern starts.

@STRING Converts a number, including decimal places, to a string.

@SUBSTRING Returns a desired portion of a string.

@TRIM Strips leading and trailing blank spaces from a string.

@UPPER Converts lowercase letters to uppercase.

@VALUE a character string with numbers into a numeric data type.

How SQLBase
Relates to
Other DBMSs

Date/time functions give you information about date/time values or provide you with a date/time result. They include:

@DATE Converts arguments to a date.

@DATETOCHAR Converts a date data type into a character data type.

@DATEVALUE Converts a string data type containing a standard date string to a date/time data type.

@DAY Returns a number between 1 and 31 that represents the day of the month.

@HOUR Returns a number between 0 and 23 that represents the hour of the day.

@MICROSECOND Returns the microsecond value in a date/time or time value.

@MINUTE Returns a number between 0 and 59 that represents the minute of the hour.

@MONTH Returns a number between 1 and 12 that represents the month of the year.

@MONTHBEG Returns the first day of the month represented by the date.

@NOW Returns the current date and time.

@QUARTER Returns a number between 1 and 4 that represents the current calendar quarter.

@QUARTERBEG Returns the date on which the current quarter began.

@SECOND Returns a number between 0 and 59 to represent the second of the minute.

@TIME Returns the current hour, minute, and second.

@TIMEVALUE Returns the date and time.

@WEEKBEG Returns the date of Monday of the week specified.

@WEEKDAY Returns a number between 0 and 6 that represents the day of the week.

@YEAR Returns a number between -1900 and +200 that represents the year relative to 1900.

@YEARBEG Returns the first day of the year represented by a date.

@YEARNO Returns a 4-digit number representing a calendar year.

Math functions perform both basic math and trigonometric operations:

@ABS Specified as @ABS(x), this function returns the absolute value of (x)

@ACOS Returns the arccosine of x.

@ASIN Returns the arcsine of x.

@ATAN Returns the arctangent of x.

@ATAN2 Returns the arctangent of y/x.

@COS Returns the cosine of x.

@EXP Returns the natural logarithmic base (e) raised to the x power.

@FACTORIAL Computes the factorial of an argument.

@INT Returns the integer portion of x.

@LN Returns the natural logarithm (base e) of (positive) x.

@LOG Returns the (positive) base-10 logarithm of x.

@MOD Returns the modulo (remainder) of x/y.

@PI Returns the value π.

@ROUND Rounds a number x with n decimal places.

@SIN Returns the sine of x.

@SQRT Returns the square root of x.

@TAN Returns the tangent of x.

How SQLBase Relates to Other DBMSs

Finance functions perform specialized math operations and include:

@CTERM Returns the number of compounding periods for an investment of present value (pv) to grow to a future value (fv), earning a fixed periodic interest rate (int).

@FV Returns the future value of a series of equal payments earning a periodic interest rate over a set number of periods.

@PMT Returns the amount of each periodic payment needed to pay off a loan principal at a periodic interest rate over a specified number of periods.

@PV Returns the present value of a series of equal payments discounted at a periodic interest rate over a set number of periods.

@RATE Returns the rate of interest for an investment of present value to grow to a future value over a set number of compounding periods.

@SLN Returns the straight-line depreciation allowance of an asset for each period, given the base cost, predicted salvage value, and expected life of the asset.

@SYD Returns the Sum-of-the-Years'-Digits depreciation allowance of an asset for a given period, given the base cost, predicted salvage value, expected life of the asset, and specific period.

@TERM Returns the number of payment periods for an investment, given the amount of each payment, the periodic interest rate, and the future value of the investment.

Logical functions return either TRUE or FALSE, depending on the value of a condition.

@IF Tests a number and returns True or False.

@ISNA Returns True if argument is Null, False for any other value.

Special functions include:

@CHOOSE Selects a value from a list based on a correlation between a selector-number and the sequence number of a value in the list.

@LICS Uses an international character set for sorting its argument, instead of the ASCII character set. It helps sort characters that are not in the English language.

Other File Server Database Systems

Although we've used SQLBase as our model from the outset, we've also mentioned other products and other approaches to combine distributed database management systems with structured query language. Taking two of the most widely known examples, dBase IV and Paradox, we can see how SQL (with the added ingredient of local area networking) can conform itself to products that weren't originally created with SQL in mind. This form of distributed processing, where databases reside on a file server, is done on individual PCs, and communications between the two is accomplished over a LAN is also known as client-based computing.

dBASE IV SQL

dBASE IV actually has two modes, one that does not use SQL and a second that does. In the first, you use specific dBASE IV commands to work on files, query the database, use Query By Example, create reports, and write and run dBASE IV programs. In the second, you use SQL to write and execute commands and run procedural language programs containing embedded SQL.

The two modes can be used together, but there are some limitations. For example, dBASE IV programs and procedures cannot contain any SQL statements; SQL programs can use most, but not all, dBASE IV commands and functions; not all dBASE IV functions (even if they can be used in SQL) can be embedded in SQL statements; SQL catalog tables are not updated in dBASE-only mode; and switching between the two modes means shutting one mode down before starting the other.

Switching back and forth between the two modes is recommended as the best way to take advantage of the respective strengths of each mode. dBase-only mode is recommended for creating screens, writing reports and creating labels, while dBASE-SQL mode is recommended for data definition and manipulation.

Paradox

A slightly different situation exists with the version of Paradox that incorporates SQL. Called Paradox SQL Link, this product is an add-on to Paradox 3.5 and is designed to let you use Paradox's traditional features while accessing data on a file server.

When you connect to a database on a server using the Paradox SQL Link, Paradox creates local versions of the database tables you want to query. You then work on these replicas using the familiar Paradox commands. When you're finished, you can update the SQL tables on the server. Convenience is the main drawing card. The initial version of the SQL Link is compatible with SQL Server, ORACLE Server 6.0, and IBM Extended Edition 1.2 Database Manager.

dBASE IV SQL and Paradox SQL Link are both workstation, or standalone PC, DBMSs that have begun to spin off variations that act, to a greater or lesser degree, as client applications to an SQL DBMS back-end. In each case, the leap into SQL is not total but the beginnings of SQL interaction are being explored.

Other File Server Database Systems

Client-Server Database Management Systems

Client-server DBMSs are the back-ends that support the client front-ends described above and do quite a bit more, besides. Applications programs like Paradox and dBASE IV usually do their own processing at the local workstations and use the central DBMS to get data and store results. Client-server DBMSs, while they can provide central databases for the front-end applications like Paradox and dBASE IV, are more often characterized as groupware products intended for use in a LAN environment and where most of the data manipulation takes place on the server instead of at the local workstation.

ORACLE and SQL Server

ORACLE is a database that runs on just about every kind of computer there is. It has a long history of shared use and development on large computer systems. Its SQL component is called SQL*PLUS. It has a special communications facility called SQL*NET that has the sole function of connecting distributed users to the DBMS. SQL Server, as we've mentioned previously, is a minicomputer program that's been moved onto PCs.

Both ORACLE and SQL Server represent the client-server architectural approach to distributed database management. Whereas Paradox SQL Link and dBASE IV SQL are clients that make relatively small use of the server DBMS, ORACLE and SQL Server are engineered to let you run all of the data manipulation processes for many users at a central location on the network. They, along with SQLBase, are software servers. The client applications create the queries in SQL and send them over the LAN to the database server (a specialized computer in the LAN that is generally dedicated to the sole task of holding and processing DBMS queries). Processing is done centrally, at the server, and the results are sent back to the client. Often, because the database server is the most powerful computer on the LAN, processing can actually take place at a faster pace. Also, because only requests and replies are transmitted over the network, the potential problem of creating bottlenecks when sending entire files back and forth over the LAN is avoided.

Client-Server Database Management Systems

Client-server database management can simplify administration in large organizations. The database administrator has only one centralized place to investigate in case of problems, and all security, backup, and recovery chores are carried out on a single machine.

A final benefit of client-server DBMSs is the fact that most of these programs, including SQLBase, SQL Server, and ORACLE, are proven applications development environments. If a commercial database applications program doesn't quite meet all of your needs, one or another of these server-based DBMSs will probably have all the tools you need to create your own custom application. Not only can such a program be designed to fill your specific needs, but when you create it with the integral DBMS, the product's own version of SQL, and its specially developed applications programming interface, it will take maximum advantage of both the client aspects and the server aspects of these database management systems.

CHECK YOURSELF

1. What is client-based computing?

2. What is client-server computing?

ANSWERS

1. Client-based computing is a form of distributed database processing in which the database program resides on the local workstation and the file server is used primarily as a storage depot.

2. Client-server computing is a form of distributed database processing in which the database program resides on the database server and local workstations are used primarily to formulate requests and display results.

QUICK SUMMARY

In this chapter we've learned about the several other varieties of SQL systems that exist. Some important points have been:

Extensions Extensions are additional statements added to standard SQL, which improve that version of SQL's ability to process and manipulate data.

Functions Functions are the data manipulation routines built into a DBMS. The database management programs generally have functions to handle such tasks as aggregate functions, math, financial data, text, logical comparisons, and date and time functions.

Client-based computing Client-based computing is a form of distributed database processing where data manipulation takes place on standalone PCs. dBASE IV SQL and Paradox SQL Link are examples.

Client-server architecture Client-server computing is a form of distributed database processing where data manipulation takes place at the central database server. SQL Server, ORACLE SQL, and SQLBase are examples.

PRACTICE WHAT YOU'VE LEARNED

1. What are the main parts of an SQL system?

2. What distinguishes SQL systems?

3. What are extensions and what purpose do they serve?

4. What is client-based computing?

5. What is client-server computing?

ANSWERS

1. SQL systems are generally composed of the DBMS (or back-end), the SQL language interface (the front-end or client), and a programming interface for one or more procedural languages (either/or precompilers and applications programming interfaces).

2. Each vendor of SQL-based DBMS systems has given a particular emphasis to the environment, the development history, and the uses to which their products will be put. Most will work in a networked environment, but some were developed with mainframes in mind, while others were specifically created for a LAN environment, and still others were developed initially for standalone PCs and have been retrofit to operate over networks.

3. Extensions are commands added to the standard SQL language to increase, improve, or refine the language's ability to manipulate data, perform queries, and control data and transactions.

4. Client-based computing is a form of distributed database processing in which the database program resides on the local workstation and the file server is used primarily as a storage depot.

5. Client-server computing is a form of distributed database processing in which the database program resides on the database server and local workstations are used primarily to formulate requests and display results.

APPENDIX
SQL Quick
Command
Reference

Chapter 10 lists the extensions that one manufacturer, Gupta Technologies, has added to its version of SQL, SQLTalk. This appendix contains those SQL statements that are standard and, therefore, a common part of all SQL variations. As you can see, the standard core of SQL is relatively small when compared with the extensions of even a single DBMS developer.

ALTER PASSWORD What the user enters to change his or her own password.

ALTER TABLE Change the description of a table.

CHECK DATABASE Integrity check command.

COMMENT ON Replace or add a comment to the description of a table, view, or column in the system catalog.

COMMIT Save all preceding transactions.

CREATE INDEX Generate an index for a particular table.

CREATE SYNONYM Give a table or view an alternate name.

CREATE TABLE Generate a table in a database.

CREATE VIEW Define a view of a table or another view.

DELETE Erase a row or rows from a table.

DROP Remove an object from a system catalog.

GRANT Give a user rights and authority levels on a table or view.

INSERT Add a row or rows to a table.

LABEL Add or change labels in catalog descriptions.

REVOKE Take away a user's rights and authority levels on a table of view.

ROLLBACK Terminate activity and lose all changes since the last COMMIT.

SELECT Query a table or view.

SAVEPOINT Assign a checkpoint within a transaction.

UNION Merge result from two or more SELECT statements.

UPDATE Update the value of columns in a table or view.

UPDATE STATISTICS Update the statistics for an index in a table.

Glossary

Aggregate function An SQL operation producing a summary value.

API Applications programming interface used by a procedural language to access an SQL database.

Argument A part of a command. It defines the data being manipulated or controls program execution.

Bind variable A variable that represents a valid value or address and associates data to an SQL command.

Cartesian product All the possible combinations of rows and columns.

Clause Part of an SQL command, begun by a keyword such as INSERT and usually containing an argument.

Column In SQL, a field or attribute. The smallest unit of data in a row.

COMMIT SQL equivalent of an application program SAVE command.

Correlated subquery A subquery that is executed repeatedly, once for each row in the main or "outer" query.

Cursor a) the position of a row within a table; b) a workspace in memory; c) an individual connection to the DBMS.

Database All of the user tables and program tables that contain data and are stored together.

Database administrator (DBA) The second highest authority in the DBMS hierarchy. Controls other users' access to the system and modifies options that affect all users.

Database object Table, view, index, synonym, or anything else created and stored in a database.

Default Any setting that is automatically assumed by the system.

Embedded SQL SQL commands used inside a procedural language program.

Equijoin Comparison of two or more columns on the basis of equality and all the columns in the tables being joined are included in the results.

Foreign key Data that logically connects two or more tables. A foreign key in one table matches the primary key of another table.

Index Data structure used to locate a row in a table without having to read the entire table.

Join A query that combines columns and data from two or more tables, or two or more columns and data from the same table.

Key Columns in an index that identify a row.

Keyword A reserved word in SQL, used as part of a command.

Nesting Placing a statement within another statement.

Operator Symbol (+, -, *, /, =, etc.) representing an operation to be performed.

Outer join A join that returns all rows, matching and nonmatching.

Outer query The main query within which nested queries reside.

Predicate Part of a search condition that sets the criteria for the search.

Primary key Column or columns that uniquely define each row in a table.

Query A database search; a request for information.

Result table Set of rows retrieved by a database search.

ROLLBACK Restore a database to its condition as of the last commit.

ROLLFORWARD Reapply changes to a database.

Row A set of related columns.

SAVEPOINT A milestone within a database transaction. An intermediate point to which you can rollback or commit.

Self-join A join that operates entirely on a single table.

Subquery A query that resides within another query.

System catalog A DBMS table that contains data about the database, rather than user data.

Table Set of columns and rows containing stored information. The basic unit of a database.

Theta join Join that uses relational operators to define the join condition.

Transaction Sequence of SQL statements forming a single unit, such as a COMMIT statement.

View A temporary (or "virtual") table made up of data from one or more base tables.

Index